Mastering Unity for Augmented Reality (AR) Development

Build Immersive AR Apps with Unity and C#

Greyson Chesterfield

COPYRIGHT

DISCLAIMER

The information provided in this book is for general informational purposes only. All content in this book reflects the author's views and is based on their research, knowledge, and experiences. The author and publisher make no representations or warranties of any kind concerning the completeness, accuracy, reliability, suitability, or availability of the information contained herein.

This book is not intended to be a substitute for professional advice, diagnosis, or treatment. Readers should seek professional advice for any specific concerns or conditions. The author and publisher disclaim any liability or responsibility for any direct, indirect, incidental, or consequential loss or damage arising from the use of the information contained in this book.

Contents

Part 1: Foundations of AR and Unity

1. Introduction to AR

What is Augmented Reality?

Augmented Reality (AR) is a technology that seamlessly blends the physical and digital worlds. Unlike virtual reality (VR), which immerses users in entirely virtual environments, AR enhances the real-world environment by overlaying digital information onto it. This interaction between the physical and virtual realms enables users to experience a richer, more interactive version of reality.

At its core, AR leverages cameras, sensors, and advanced algorithms to map the real world and place virtual objects or information within that space. The defining features of AR include:

1. **Real-Time Interaction**: Digital overlays respond to user movements and inputs in real-time.

2. **Spatial Awareness**: AR systems can recognize and interact with physical objects and environments.

3. **Enhanced Perception**: By superimposing virtual data—such as text, images, or 3D models—AR provides information and

experiences that would otherwise be inaccessible.

The Appeal of AR

The allure of AR lies in its ability to make interactions more immersive and intuitive. Whether enabling users to see how a piece of furniture fits in their living room or offering interactive tutorials for complex machinery, AR transforms how we perceive and interact with information.

The Current Landscape: AR in Gaming, Healthcare, Retail, and Education

AR is not a futuristic technology; it is here, transforming industries worldwide. Let's explore its current applications:

1. Gaming

Gaming is arguably the most visible and widely embraced use case for AR. By combining the physical and digital realms, AR revolutionizes gameplay, making it more engaging and interactive. A standout example is **Pokémon Go**, a game that became a cultural phenomenon by allowing players to "catch" Pokémon in their real-world surroundings.

AR gaming extends beyond entertainment:

- Multiplayer AR games promote social interaction.

- Geolocation-based mechanics encourage physical activity.

2. Healthcare

In the healthcare sector, AR empowers both professionals and patients by providing visual aids and tools for diagnostics, surgery, and rehabilitation. Key applications include:

- **Surgical Training and Assistance**: AR allows surgeons to visualize internal organs and structures without invasive procedures, enhancing precision.

- **Patient Education**: AR-enabled apps help patients understand complex medical conditions and treatments.

- **Physical Therapy**: AR games and activities motivate patients during rehabilitation.

3. Retail

Retailers leverage AR to create personalized and engaging shopping experiences:

- **Virtual Try-Ons**: Apps like **IKEA Place** and **Sephora Virtual Artist** allow customers to see how products look in their homes or on their bodies.

- **Interactive Displays**: AR-powered kiosks in stores provide detailed product information or create gamified shopping experiences.

- **Customer Engagement**: AR campaigns, such as treasure hunts or interactive ads, foster brand loyalty.

4. Education

In education, AR bridges the gap between abstract concepts and tangible understanding:

- **Interactive Learning**: AR apps bring subjects like biology, astronomy, and history to life by allowing students to explore 3D models of cells, planets, or historical landmarks.

- **Skill Training**: Fields such as engineering and aviation use AR simulations to train professionals in a risk-free environment.

AR's Broader Potential

Beyond these domains, AR is also making strides in manufacturing (e.g., assembly line guidance), real estate (virtual property walkthroughs), and even entertainment (immersive storytelling experiences).

Examples of AR in Action

Let's take a closer look at some real-world examples that highlight AR's versatility and impact:

1. Pokémon Go

Released in 2016, Pokémon Go is a hallmark of AR's potential to engage users at scale. The game superimposes virtual creatures onto real-world environments, encouraging players to explore their surroundings. With its simple yet addictive mechanics, Pokémon Go showed how AR could blend entertainment with physical activity, social connection, and exploration.

2. IKEA Place

This app lets users visualize how furniture will look in their homes before making a purchase. By using AR, IKEA eliminates uncertainty and enhances the shopping experience. Customers can scale, rotate, and move furniture within their spaces, making the app both practical and innovative.

3. Snapchat Filters

Snapchat popularized AR filters, which apply virtual effects to real-world photos and videos in real time. From playful overlays like dog ears to more sophisticated filters that alter backgrounds or appearances, these features have redefined how people interact with social media.

Why Unity for AR?

Unity has emerged as the leading platform for developing AR applications. Here's why it's the go-to choice for AR developers:

1. Cross-Platform Compatibility

Unity's ability to deploy applications across multiple platforms—iOS, Android, Windows, and more—is invaluable for AR development. This flexibility ensures that apps can reach a wide audience without requiring extensive rework for each platform.

2. AR Foundation

Unity's AR Foundation is a robust framework that abstracts the complexities of working with ARCore (Android) and ARKit (iOS). It provides developers with a unified set of tools for:

- Plane detection
- Image recognition
- Environmental tracking
- Object placement

3. Real-Time Rendering

Unity's real-time rendering engine is optimized for creating visually stunning AR experiences. Its capabilities allow developers to integrate realistic lighting, shadows, and physics into their projects, ensuring that virtual objects blend seamlessly with the real world.

4. Rich Asset Store

Unity's Asset Store offers a treasure trove of ready-made assets, including 3D models, animations, and scripts. This ecosystem accelerates development by reducing the time and effort needed to create custom assets.

5. C# Scripting

Unity uses C# as its primary programming language. With its clear syntax and extensive documentation, C# is beginner-friendly yet powerful enough for complex AR applications.

6. Developer Community and Support

Unity boasts a vast and active developer community. From forums and tutorials to dedicated AR development resources, developers can find solutions to almost any challenge.

7. Proven Track Record

Unity has been the backbone of many successful AR applications, from games like Pokémon Go to enterprise tools for training and simulation. This track record provides confidence in its reliability and scalability.

AR is a transformative technology reshaping how we interact with the world around us. From games to healthcare, its applications are as diverse as they are impactful. Unity's robust tools and resources make it the ideal platform for developers eager to dive into AR development. As we embark on this journey together, you'll learn not just how to build AR applications but also how to make them engaging, intuitive, and ready for the real world.

The next chapter will guide you through setting up your development environment, turning the abstract promise of AR into something you can see, touch, and experience. Let's begin!

2. Setting Up Your Environment

Setting up your development environment is the crucial first step toward creating immersive AR applications with Unity. This chapter will guide you through installing Unity, understanding its interface, configuring AR tools and libraries, and building your first "Hello AR World" project.

Installing Unity and Understanding Its Interface

Installing Unity

Unity is a powerful and flexible game engine, widely used for AR development. Follow these steps to install Unity:

1. **Download the Unity Hub**:
   - Unity Hub is a centralized application for managing Unity installations and projects. Visit Unity's official website and download the Unity Hub.

2. **Install the Unity Editor**:

   o Open Unity Hub and navigate to the **Installs** tab.

   o Click **Add** and select the version of Unity you want to install. For AR development, choose a version that supports **AR Foundation** (2021 or later is recommended).

3. **Select Required Modules**:

   o During installation, select the following modules:

     ▪ Android Build Support

     ▪ iOS Build Support

     ▪ Windows Build Support (if targeting Windows devices)

4. **Create a Unity Account**:

   o Sign in or create a Unity account. This step is necessary for activating the Unity license, which is free for individual developers and small businesses.

Understanding the Unity Interface

Once installed, launch Unity and create a new project. You'll encounter the Unity Editor interface, which comprises several key components:

1. **Scene View**:

   o This is where you build and arrange your AR scene. Think of it as the virtual workspace for your app.

2. **Game View**:

   o The Game View shows a preview of your app as it will appear to users.

3. **Hierarchy Panel**:

   o This panel lists all the GameObjects in your scene, such as 3D models, lights, and cameras.

4. **Inspector Panel**:

   o Here, you can configure the properties of selected GameObjects, such as their size, position, or behavior.

5. **Project Panel**:

   o This panel displays all the assets (e.g., scripts, models, textures) in your project.

6. **Console**:

   o The Console logs messages, errors, and warnings, helping you debug your project.

Understanding these panels and how they interact is essential for effective development in Unity.

Unity's AR Foundation: Bridging ARCore and ARKit

Unity's **AR Foundation** simplifies AR development by providing a unified framework for working with both **ARCore** (Android) and **ARKit** (iOS). This abstraction layer allows you to write code once and deploy it on multiple platforms.

Key Features of AR Foundation

- **Plane Detection**: Detect horizontal and vertical surfaces in the real world.

- **Anchor Points**: Enable objects to "stick" to a specific location in the real-world environment.

- **Image Recognition**: Identify and track images, such as posters or QR codes.

- **Environmental Understanding**: Use depth information for occlusion (where virtual objects appear behind real-world objects).

Installing AR Foundation

1. Open Unity and navigate to **Window > Package Manager**.

2. Search for **AR Foundation** and install it.

3. Depending on your target platforms, also install:

- ○ **ARCore XR Plugin** for Android.

- ○ **ARKit XR Plugin** for iOS.

These packages provide platform-specific functionality while remaining compatible with AR Foundation's API.

Necessary Tools and Libraries

To build and test AR applications, you'll need additional tools and libraries:

1. Visual Studio

- **What is Visual Studio?**

  - ○ Visual Studio is an integrated development environment (IDE) used to write, edit, and debug C# scripts in Unity.

- **Installation**:

  - ○ Download and install Visual Studio Community Edition (free) from Visual Studio's website.

- During installation, ensure the **Game Development with Unity** workload is selected.

2. Android Setup

To build AR apps for Android devices:

1. **Install Android SDK and NDK**:
   - Unity includes these tools, but you must enable them during Unity installation or later in Unity Hub under **Installs > Add Modules**.

2. **Enable Developer Mode on Your Android Device**:
   - Go to **Settings > About Phone** and tap the Build Number seven times to enable Developer Mode.
   - Enable **USB Debugging** in Developer Options.

3. **Connect Your Device**:
   - Connect your Android device to your computer via USB. Unity will detect it during builds.

3. iOS Setup

To build AR apps for iOS devices:

1. **Install Xcode**:

   o Xcode is required to build iOS apps. Download it from the Mac App Store.

2. **Set Up an Apple Developer Account**:

   o Sign up at Apple Developer. A paid membership is required for app deployment.

3. **Configure Your iOS Device**:

   o Connect your iPhone or iPad to your Mac. Use Xcode to manage device provisioning.

A Quick-Start Guide: Your First "Hello AR World" Project

Let's create a simple AR project that places a virtual cube on a detected surface.

Step 1: Set Up the Project

1. Open Unity and create a new 3D project.

2. Navigate to **File > Build Settings** and select your target platform (Android or iOS). Click **Switch Platform**.

Step 2: Configure AR Foundation

1. Open **Edit > Project Settings** and enable:

- XR Plug-in Management.

- Select the appropriate AR plugins (ARCore for Android, ARKit for iOS).

2. Add a **AR Session Origin** and **AR Session** GameObject to your scene:

   - Right-click in the **Hierarchy** panel and choose **XR > AR Session Origin**. This controls the camera and AR coordinate space.

   - Add an **AR Session** for managing AR-specific functionality.

Step 3: Add a Virtual Object

1. Create a **Cube**:

   - Right-click in the **Hierarchy** panel and choose **3D Object > Cube**.

2. Position the cube:

   - Set its initial position to (0, 0, 0) relative to the AR camera.

Step 4: Write a Simple Script

1. Create a new C# script called PlaceOnPlane and attach it to your AR Session Origin.

2. In the script, implement functionality to detect surfaces and place the cube:

- o Use **AR Raycast Manager** for detecting planes.

- o On a tap gesture, instantiate the cube at the detected location.

Step 5: Build and Test

1. Connect your device to your computer.

2. Navigate to **File > Build Settings** and click **Build and Run**.

3. Deploy the app to your device and test it by pointing the camera at a flat surface.

Setting up your environment is the first hands-on step in your AR development journey. With Unity, AR Foundation, and the necessary tools configured, you've built a foundation for creating immersive AR experiences. Your "Hello AR World" project is just the beginning—this simple cube placement app demonstrates how quickly AR can connect the virtual and real worlds.

Next, we'll dive deeper into Unity's core concepts and explore how to make AR objects interactive and engaging. Let's build!

3. Understanding ARCore, ARKit, and AR Foundation

Augmented Reality (AR) development requires tools that bridge the gap between the physical and virtual worlds. Two leading AR software development kits (SDKs) are **ARCore** for Android and **ARKit** for iOS. While these SDKs are platform-specific, Unity's **AR Foundation** provides a unified interface for building AR applications across platforms.

This chapter explores the strengths of ARCore and ARKit, explains how AR Foundation simplifies cross-platform AR development, and guides you through a real-world example: **surface detection using AR Foundation.**

What ARCore (Android) and ARKit (iOS) Bring to the Table

ARCore and ARKit are the backbone of AR applications on Android and iOS, respectively. They provide developers with tools to create immersive AR experiences by leveraging device hardware like cameras, accelerometers, and depth sensors.

ARCore: Google's AR SDK for Android

ARCore was introduced by Google to enable AR experiences on Android devices. It works by combining three key capabilities:

1. **Motion Tracking**:
   - ARCore uses the device's camera and inertial sensors to understand its position in 3D space. This allows it to track the user's movement and adjust the AR environment accordingly.

2. **Environmental Understanding**:
   - ARCore detects horizontal and vertical surfaces, such as floors, tables, and walls, where virtual objects can be placed.

3. **Light Estimation**:
   - ARCore analyzes ambient lighting in the real-world environment to match the brightness and shadows of virtual objects, making them appear more realistic.

ARCore Highlights

- Broad device compatibility across Android smartphones and tablets.

- Advanced features like depth API for occlusion and better surface understanding.

- Support for geospatial tracking (e.g., anchoring objects to specific GPS coordinates).

ARKit: Apple's AR SDK for iOS

ARKit, developed by Apple, offers similar functionality for iOS devices. It is tightly integrated with Apple's hardware and software ecosystem, allowing for optimized performance and unique features.

1. **World Tracking**:

   o ARKit uses Visual Inertial Odometry (VIO) to track device movement and map the physical environment.

2. **Scene Understanding**:

   o ARKit recognizes surfaces, detects objects, and even maps complex 3D environments.

3. **Light Estimation and HDR Support**:

   o ARKit includes advanced light estimation and High Dynamic Range

(HDR) rendering for hyper-realistic visuals.

4. **Face Tracking**:

    o   ARKit supports face tracking on devices with TrueDepth cameras, enabling AR experiences like virtual makeup or facial animations.

ARKit Highlights

- Exclusive features like body tracking and motion capture.

- Seamless integration with Apple hardware (LiDAR sensors on iPhone Pro models).

- Performance optimization through Metal, Apple's graphics framework.

How Unity's AR Foundation Unifies These SDKs

Developing separate applications for Android and iOS can be a daunting task, especially when each platform has unique APIs, capabilities, and limitations. Unity's **AR Foundation** addresses this challenge by providing a single interface that works across ARCore and ARKit.

Benefits of AR Foundation

1. **Unified Workflow**:

   o AR Foundation abstracts the differences between ARCore and ARKit, allowing developers to write code once and deploy it to both platforms. For example, surface detection uses the same methods and events, regardless of the target platform.

2. **Cross-Platform Support**:

   o By supporting both ARCore and ARKit, AR Foundation ensures your app reaches a broader audience with minimal additional effort.

3. **Feature Parity**:

   o AR Foundation exposes the most common AR features provided by ARCore and ARKit:

     ▪ Plane detection

     ▪ Image tracking

     ▪ Depth sensing

     ▪ Anchoring

4. **Customizability**:

   o Developers can add platform-specific features when needed. For example, you can access ARKit's advanced facial tracking or ARCore's geospatial API while still benefiting from AR Foundation's unified structure.

How AR Foundation Works

AR Foundation is built on Unity's XR (Extended Reality) framework and communicates with ARCore and ARKit through platform-specific plugins:

- **ARCore XR Plugin**: Connects AR Foundation to ARCore.

- **ARKit XR Plugin**: Connects AR Foundation to ARKit.

By configuring Unity's **XR Plug-in Management**, you can enable both plugins and let AR Foundation handle the underlying SDK interactions.

Real-World Example: Surface Detection Using AR Foundation

Now that you understand the tools, let's implement a practical example: detecting surfaces in the physical environment using AR Foundation.

Objective

We'll build an app that detects horizontal surfaces and allows the user to place a virtual object, such as a 3D cube, on them.

Step 1: Project Setup

1. **Create a New Unity Project**:

   o Open Unity and create a new 3D project.

   o Navigate to **File > Build Settings** and select your target platform (Android or iOS). Click **Switch Platform**.

2. **Install AR Foundation**:

   o Open the **Package Manager** (Window > Package Manager).

   o Search for and install the following packages:

      ▪ **AR Foundation**

      ▪ **ARCore XR Plugin** (for Android)

      ▪ **ARKit XR Plugin** (for iOS)

3. **Enable XR Plug-in Management**:

   o Go to **Edit > Project Settings > XR Plug-in Management** and enable ARCore or ARKit, depending on your platform.

Step 2: Scene Configuration

1. **Add AR Session and AR Session Origin**:

- In the **Hierarchy** panel, right-click and select **XR > AR Session Origin**.
    - **AR Session Origin** handles the camera and AR interactions.
    - **AR Camera** is automatically added and configured.
- Add an **AR Session** to manage the lifecycle of AR features.

2. **Add an AR Plane Manager**:
    - Select the **AR Session Origin** GameObject.
    - Click **Add Component** and search for **AR Plane Manager**.
        - The AR Plane Manager detects surfaces and tracks their boundaries.

3. **Add AR Raycast Manager**:
    - Still on **AR Session Origin**, add the **AR Raycast Manager** component.
        - This allows the app to cast rays into the physical environment and detect where surfaces are located.

4. **Visualize Detected Planes**:
    - Create a material for the planes:

- Right-click in the **Assets** folder and select **Create > Material**. Assign it a semi-transparent color.

  o In the AR Plane Manager component, assign this material to **Plane Prefab**.

Step 3: Adding a Virtual Object

1. **Create a 3D Object**:

   o In the **Hierarchy** panel, right-click and select **3D Object > Cube**.

   o Position the cube at (0, 0, 0).

2. **Make the Object Movable**:

   o Create a script called PlaceOnPlane:

     - Right-click in the **Assets** folder, choose **Create > C# Script**, and name it PlaceOnPlane.

   o Attach the script to the **AR Session Origin**.

Step 4: Writing the Script

Below is the logic for detecting surfaces and placing the cube:

csharp

```
Copy code
using UnityEngine;
using UnityEngine.XR.ARFoundation;
using UnityEngine.XR.ARSubsystems;
using System.Collections.Generic;

public class PlaceOnPlane : MonoBehaviour
{
    public GameObject placedObject; // Assign the cube here.
    private ARRaycastManager raycastManager;
    private List<ARRaycastHit> hits = new List<ARRaycastHit>();

    void Start()
    {
        raycastManager = GetComponent<ARRaycastManager>();
    }

    void Update()
    {
```

```csharp
if (Input.touchCount > 0)

{

    Touch touch = Input.GetTouch(0);


    if (raycastManager.Raycast(touch.position,
hits, TrackableType.PlaneWithinPolygon))
    {
        Pose hitPose = hits[0].pose;
        if (placedObject == null)
        {
            placedObject = Instantiate(placedObject,
hitPose.position, hitPose.rotation);
        }
        else
        {
            placedObject.transform.position =
hitPose.position;
        }
    }
}
}
```

This script:

- Detects when the user taps on a surface.

- Raycasts to find the surface position.

- Places or moves the cube to the detected location.

Step 5: Build and Test

1. Connect your device to your computer.

2. Navigate to **File > Build Settings** and click **Build and Run**.

3. Test the app:

   o Point the camera at a flat surface, and the app will detect it.

   o Tap on the screen to place the cube.

ARCore and ARKit are powerful SDKs for building platform-specific AR applications, but Unity's AR Foundation bridges the gap, allowing developers to create cross-platform experiences effortlessly. By leveraging AR Foundation, you can focus on building compelling AR content without worrying about platform-specific implementation details.

The surface detection example you just implemented is foundational to many AR applications, from virtual furniture placement to AR gaming. In the next chapter, we'll dive deeper into Unity's core features for creating interactive and visually engaging AR experiences.

Part 2: Core Concepts in Unity for AR

4. Unity Basics for AR

To master AR development, it's essential to understand Unity's fundamental building blocks. GameObjects, Components, Prefabs, Scenes, and Hierarchies are at the core of every Unity project. This chapter will guide you through these concepts and how they relate to AR, setting the stage with a practical example of placing a 3D object on a real-world surface.

GameObjects, Components, and Prefabs

GameObjects

In Unity, **GameObjects** are the fundamental units of every scene. Think of a GameObject as an empty container that can represent anything in your project: a 3D model, a light source, or even a logical placeholder.

- **Examples in AR**:
    - A virtual chair in an AR furniture app.
    - An invisible raycasting tool for detecting surfaces.

o A camera representing the user's point of view.

GameObjects themselves don't have any behavior or functionality until you add **Components** to them.

Components

Components define the behavior and properties of a GameObject. By attaching components, you can make GameObjects move, rotate, detect collisions, or display visuals.

- **Common Components**:
  - **Transform**: Every GameObject has a Transform component that specifies its position, rotation, and scale.
  - **Mesh Renderer**: Displays the 3D model of the GameObject.
  - **Collider**: Defines the physical boundaries for detecting interactions.
  - **Scripts**: Custom C# scripts add specific behaviors to GameObjects, such as responding to user input.

- **AR-Specific Components**:
  - **AR Plane Manager**: Detects and tracks real-world surfaces.
  - **AR Raycast Manager**: Casts virtual rays to interact with the environment.

Prefabs

A **Prefab** is a reusable GameObject blueprint. Once you create a Prefab, you can instantiate (spawn) it multiple times in your scene. This is particularly useful in AR, where virtual objects like furniture or characters need to be dynamically placed.

- **Example**: A Prefab for a virtual cube can be reused every time a user taps on a detected surface to place it in the scene.

Scenes and Hierarchies

Scenes

A **Scene** in Unity is like a container that holds everything in your AR app at a specific point in time. In AR projects, a Scene might represent:

- The main AR experience.

- A menu or splash screen.

- A tutorial space.

Scenes can contain multiple GameObjects, including AR-specific managers like cameras and light sources.

Hierarchy

The **Hierarchy Panel** lists all the GameObjects in your Scene, organized in a tree structure. This structure reflects the relationships between GameObjects:

- **Parent-Child Relationships**:

  o A parent GameObject can have child objects. For example, an AR Session Origin (parent) might have a Camera (child).

  o Transforming a parent (e.g., moving it) also affects its children.

Organizing the Hierarchy helps you manage complex AR applications effectively.

Lights, Cameras, and Action: The Essentials for AR Apps

Lights

Lighting is crucial for making virtual objects blend seamlessly into the real world. Unity provides several lighting options:

- **Directional Light**:

  o Represents sunlight or a consistent light source.

- o Often used in AR apps to mimic real-world lighting.

- **Point Light**:

  - o Emits light from a single point, like a light bulb.

- **Spotlight**:

  - o Projects a cone of light, similar to a flashlight.

AR-Specific Lighting: Unity's AR Foundation supports **light estimation**, which adjusts the lighting of virtual objects to match the real-world environment.

Cameras

In AR, the camera is the user's window into the augmented experience. Unity's AR Foundation automatically configures the AR camera:

- Captures the real-world environment using the device's camera.

- Renders virtual objects over the physical world.

- Adjusts field of view and depth for realistic interaction.

The **AR Camera** in Unity is a specialized version of a standard Unity camera, equipped with components for handling AR functionality.

Real-World Example: Placing a 3D Object on a Real-World Surface

Let's apply the concepts of GameObjects, Components, Prefabs, and lighting in a practical example.

Objective

Create an AR app where a user can tap on a detected surface to place a 3D object (a virtual cube) in the real world.

Step 1: Setting Up the Scene

1. **Create a New Unity Project**:

    o   Open Unity and create a new 3D project.

    o   Set the platform to Android or iOS in **File > Build Settings**.

2. **Add AR Session and AR Session Origin**:

    o   Right-click in the **Hierarchy** and select **XR > AR Session Origin**.

    o   This adds an **AR Camera** and sets up AR functionality for detecting surfaces.

3. **Add Plane Detection**:

- ○ Select the **AR Session Origin** in the Hierarchy.

- ○ Add the **AR Plane Manager** component via the Inspector panel.

  - ▪ The AR Plane Manager will detect and track horizontal surfaces.

4. **Add a Raycast Manager**:

   - ○ Still on the **AR Session Origin**, add the **AR Raycast Manager** component.

     - ▪ This will allow you to detect where the user taps on a surface.

5. **Create a Material for Planes**:

   - ○ Right-click in the **Assets** folder and select **Create > Material**.

   - ○ Assign a semi-transparent color for better visibility of detected surfaces.

   - ○ Set this material as the **Plane Prefab** in the AR Plane Manager.

Step 2: Adding a Virtual Object

1. **Create a 3D Cube**:

   - ○ Right-click in the Hierarchy and select **3D Object > Cube**.

- Adjust its size to make it smaller (e.g., 0.1 units on each axis).

2. **Create a Prefab**:

   - Drag the Cube from the Hierarchy into the **Assets** folder to create a Prefab.

   - Delete the original Cube from the Scene (it will be instantiated dynamically).

Step 3: Writing the Placement Script

Create a new script to handle user interactions and place the cube on detected surfaces.

1. **Create a Script**:

   - Right-click in the Assets folder, select **Create > C# Script**, and name it PlaceObjectOnSurface.

2. **Add the Following Code**:

csharp

Copy code

```csharp
using UnityEngine;

using UnityEngine.XR.ARFoundation;

using UnityEngine.XR.ARSubsystems;

using System.Collections.Generic;
```

```csharp
public class PlaceObjectOnSurface : MonoBehaviour
{
    public GameObject objectPrefab; // Assign the Cube
    prefab in the Inspector

    private ARRaycastManager raycastManager;

    private List<ARRaycastHit> hits = new
    List<ARRaycastHit>();

    void Start()
    {
        raycastManager =
    GetComponent<ARRaycastManager>();
    }

    void Update()
    {
        if (Input.touchCount > 0)
        {
            Touch touch = Input.GetTouch(0);

            if (touch.phase == TouchPhase.Began)
            {
```

```
            if (raycastManager.Raycast(touch.position,
hits, TrackableType.PlaneWithinPolygon))

                {

                    Pose hitPose = hits[0].pose;

                    Instantiate(objectPrefab, hitPose.position,
hitPose.rotation);

                }

            }

        }

    }

}
```

3. **Attach the Script**:

   o Attach the PlaceObjectOnSurface script
      to the **AR Session Origin** GameObject.

   o Assign the Cube Prefab to the Object
      Prefab field in the Inspector.

Step 4: Adding Realistic Lighting

1. **Add a Directional Light**:

   o Right-click in the Hierarchy, select **Light
      > Directional Light**.

   o Position and rotate the light to simulate
      natural sunlight.

2. **Enable Light Estimation**:

   o   In the AR Session Origin, enable light
       estimation in the AR Camera Manager
       component to match real-world lighting
       conditions.

Step 5: Build and Test

1. Connect your device to your computer.

2. Go to **File > Build Settings** and click **Build
   and Run**.

3. Point the camera at a flat surface, and tap to
   place the virtual cube.

This example demonstrates how GameObjects,
Components, and Prefabs form the foundation of Unity
AR development. By integrating AR-specific tools like
the AR Raycast Manager and Plane Manager, you can
bring virtual objects into the real world interactively.

5. Building AR Interaction Models

Creating engaging AR applications requires dynamic and intuitive interaction models. This chapter explores how to handle gestures, use raycasting for connecting virtual objects with the real world, and implement anchors for object persistence. We'll conclude with a practical example: building a draggable AR object.

Handling Touch Gestures: Tap, Swipe, and Pinch

Touch gestures are the primary way users interact with AR applications. Unity provides tools to recognize and respond to these gestures.

1. Tap Gesture

The tap gesture is the most basic interaction. It's typically used to select or place virtual objects.

- **Implementation in AR**:
    - Detect a tap using Input.GetTouch().
    - Use raycasting to determine if the tap intersects with a virtual object or surface.

2. Swipe Gesture

Swiping is a directional movement, often used for scrolling, rotating, or navigating.

- **Implementation in AR**:

    ○ Track the start and end positions of a touch.

    ○ Calculate the swipe direction and velocity to perform the desired action.

3. Pinch Gesture

Pinching is a multi-touch gesture used for scaling or zooming objects.

- **Implementation in AR**:

    ○ Detect two simultaneous touch points.

    ○ Measure the distance between the touch points and adjust the scale of the virtual object accordingly.

Unity Example: Gesture Detection

Here's how you can detect a simple tap in Unity:

csharp

Copy code

```
if (Input.touchCount > 0)
{
    Touch touch = Input.GetTouch(0);
```

```
if (touch.phase == TouchPhase.Began)

    {

        Debug.Log("Screen tapped at position: " +
touch.position);

    }

}
```

You can extend this logic to detect swipes and pinches by monitoring touch positions and movements.

Raycasting: Connecting Virtual Objects with the Real World

Raycasting is a technique where a virtual "ray" is cast from the camera or user's touch point into the AR environment. It is used to:

- Detect surfaces.

- Interact with objects.

- Place virtual elements accurately.

AR Raycast Manager

Unity's **AR Raycast Manager** simplifies raycasting in AR. It detects planes or features in the environment and provides the world coordinates of the hit point.

Using Raycasting for Placement

Here's a script for placing an object on a detected surface using raycasting:

csharp

Copy code

```csharp
using UnityEngine;

using UnityEngine.XR.ARFoundation;

using UnityEngine.XR.ARSubsystems;

using System.Collections.Generic;


public class RaycastPlacement : MonoBehaviour
{
    public GameObject objectToPlace;

    private ARRaycastManager raycastManager;

    private List<ARRaycastHit> hits = new List<ARRaycastHit>();


    void Start()
    {
        raycastManager = GetComponent<ARRaycastManager>();
    }
```

```
void Update()
{
    if (Input.touchCount > 0)
    {
        Touch touch = Input.GetTouch(0);

        if (touch.phase == TouchPhase.Began)
        {
            if (raycastManager.Raycast(touch.position,
hits, TrackableType.PlaneWithinPolygon))
            {
                Pose hitPose = hits[0].pose;
                Instantiate(objectToPlace,
hitPose.position, hitPose.rotation);
            }
        }
    }
}
```

This script places an object at the intersection of the ray and a detected surface.

Anchors and Persistence: Making AR Objects "Stick"

In AR, anchors are used to ensure virtual objects stay in place, even when the user moves the device. Without anchors, objects might shift or disappear due to tracking errors.

What Are Anchors?

Anchors are points in the physical world that maintain their position and orientation relative to detected surfaces. They are critical for:

- Creating stable and believable AR experiences.

- Saving and restoring AR scenes.

Implementing Anchors in Unity

Unity's **AR Anchor Manager** manages anchors for AR applications. Here's how to use it:

1. Add the **AR Anchor Manager** component to the AR Session Origin.

2. Attach virtual objects to anchors when placing them.

Example:

csharp

Copy code

```
ARAnchorManager anchorManager =
GetComponent<ARAnchorManager>();


if (raycastManager.Raycast(touch.position, hits,
TrackableType.PlaneWithinPolygon))
{
    Pose hitPose = hits[0].pose;
    ARAnchor anchor =
anchorManager.AddAnchor(hitPose);
    if (anchor != null)
    {
        Instantiate(objectToPlace, anchor.transform);
    }
}
```

Real-World Example: Creating a Draggable AR Object

Let's put it all together to create a draggable AR object. The app will allow users to tap and drag an object across a detected surface.

Objective

Enable users to tap on a virtual object and drag it to a new location.

Step 1: Setting Up the Scene

1. **Create a New Project**:

   o Open Unity and create a new 3D project.

2. **Add AR Session and AR Session Origin**:

   o Right-click in the **Hierarchy** and select **XR > AR Session Origin**.

   o Add **AR Session** to manage AR functionality.

3. **Add Plane Detection**:

   o Select the **AR Session Origin** and add the **AR Plane Manager** and **AR Raycast Manager** components.

Step 2: Creating the Draggable Object

1. **Create a 3D Cube**:

   o Right-click in the **Hierarchy** and select **3D Object > Cube**.

   o Adjust its size and position.

2. **Create a Prefab**:

- Drag the Cube into the **Assets** folder to create a Prefab.

Step 3: Writing the Drag Script

Create a script to handle dragging:

1. **Create a Script**:
   - Right-click in the Assets folder, select **Create > C# Script**, and name it DraggableObject.

2. **Add the Following Code**:

csharp

Copy code

```
using UnityEngine;

using UnityEngine.XR.ARFoundation;

using UnityEngine.XR.ARSubsystems;

using System.Collections.Generic;


public class DraggableObject : MonoBehaviour

{

    private ARRaycastManager raycastManager;

    private List<ARRaycastHit> hits = new
List<ARRaycastHit>();
```

```csharp
private Camera arCamera;
private bool isDragging = false;

void Start()
{
    raycastManager =
FindObjectOfType<ARRaycastManager>();
    arCamera = Camera.main;
}

void Update()
{
    if (Input.touchCount == 0) return;

    Touch touch = Input.GetTouch(0);

    if (touch.phase == TouchPhase.Began)
    {
        Ray ray =
arCamera.ScreenPointToRay(touch.position);
        RaycastHit hit;
```

```csharp
            if (Physics.Raycast(ray, out hit) &&
hit.transform == transform)
            {
                isDragging = true;
            }
        }
        else if (touch.phase == TouchPhase.Moved &&
isDragging)
        {
            if (raycastManager.Raycast(touch.position,
hits, TrackableType.PlaneWithinPolygon))
            {
                Pose hitPose = hits[0].pose;

                transform.position = hitPose.position;
            }
        }
        else if (touch.phase == TouchPhase.Ended)
        {
            isDragging = false;
        }
    }
}
```

This script:

- Detects when the user taps on the object.

- Enables dragging by updating the object's position to match the raycast hit position.

Step 4: Testing the Application

1. **Assign the Script**:
   - Attach the DraggableObject script to the Cube Prefab.
   - Ensure the Cube has a Collider component for detecting touch interactions.

2. **Deploy to a Device**:
   - Build and run the project on an Android or iOS device.
   - Test by dragging the cube across a detected surface.

This chapter explored essential AR interaction models, from handling gestures and raycasting to using anchors for persistence. By combining these techniques, you can create dynamic and intuitive AR applications. The draggable AR object demonstrates how these concepts work together, enabling users to interact naturally with virtual content.

6. Understanding AR Features

AR development thrives on its ability to blend the virtual and real worlds seamlessly. Unity's AR Foundation provides developers with robust tools for features like plane detection, image recognition, and environmental understanding, enabling immersive and interactive experiences. In this chapter, we'll explore these features in-depth and apply them to a real-world example: creating an AR measuring tool.

Plane Detection and Tracking

Plane detection is a foundational feature in AR, enabling apps to identify flat surfaces like floors, tables, and walls in the real-world environment.

How It Works

AR plane detection involves analyzing camera data to detect areas of consistent color and texture that likely correspond to flat surfaces. Once detected, AR systems generate a "virtual plane" that overlays the physical surface.

- **Horizontal Planes**: Detect tables, floors, or other flat surfaces parallel to the ground.

- **Vertical Planes**: Detect walls or upright surfaces.

Unity's AR Plane Manager

In Unity, the **AR Plane Manager** component handles plane detection. It:

- Tracks detected planes in real time.

- Updates the boundaries of planes as the user moves.

- Generates plane GameObjects for visualization or interaction.

Example: Visualizing Detected Planes

To visualize detected planes in Unity:

1. Add the AR Plane Manager to the **AR Session Origin**.

2. Create a transparent material for the planes.

3. Assign this material to the **Plane Prefab** property in the AR Plane Manager.

csharp

Copy code

```csharp
public class PlaneVisualization : MonoBehaviour
{
    private ARPlaneManager planeManager;
```

```
void Start()

{

    planeManager =
FindObjectOfType<ARPlaneManager>();

    foreach (ARPlane plane in
planeManager.trackables)

    {

plane.GetComponent<MeshRenderer>().material =
customMaterial;

    }

  }

}
```

This approach helps users understand the app's detected AR space, improving interaction.

Image Recognition and Markers

Image recognition allows AR applications to identify and track specific images in the environment, such as posters, logos, or QR codes. This feature is useful for:

- Launching interactive experiences tied to specific images.

- Triggering animations or displaying information when a recognized image is detected.

Unity's AR Tracked Image Manager

The **AR Tracked Image Manager** component handles image recognition in Unity. It matches detected images in the environment with reference images stored in an image library.

How to Use AR Tracked Image Manager

1. Create a Reference Image Library:

   o Go to the **Assets** folder, right-click, and select **Create > XR > Reference Image Library**.

   o Add images you want to recognize and assign unique identifiers to each.

2. Attach the AR Tracked Image Manager:

   o Add the AR Tracked Image Manager to the **AR Session Origin**.

   o Assign the Reference Image Library to it.

Example: Responding to Recognized Images

Here's a script to instantiate a virtual object when an image is recognized:

```csharp
csharp

Copy code

using UnityEngine;

using UnityEngine.XR.ARFoundation;


public class ImageRecognitionHandler :
MonoBehaviour
{
    public GameObject objectToSpawn;

    private ARTrackedImageManager imageManager;


    void Start()
    {
        imageManager =
FindObjectOfType<ARTrackedImageManager>();

        imageManager.trackedImagesChanged +=
OnTrackedImagesChanged;

    }


    void
OnTrackedImagesChanged(ARTrackedImagesChange
dEventArgs args)
```

```
{
    foreach (ARTrackedImage trackedImage in
args.added)
    {
        Instantiate(objectToSpawn,
trackedImage.transform.position, Quaternion.identity);
    }
}
}
```

This code spawns an object at the location of the recognized image.

Environmental Understanding: Depth and Occlusion

Environmental understanding enhances realism in AR by considering the depth of real-world objects and how virtual objects interact with them.

Depth Sensing

Depth sensing measures the distance between the camera and objects in the environment. It's essential for:

- Accurately placing virtual objects in the scene.

- Avoiding collisions between virtual and real objects.

Depth API in ARCore

Unity supports ARCore's Depth API, which uses depth sensors and camera data to estimate the spatial relationship between objects.

Occlusion

Occlusion occurs when real-world objects block virtual ones. Without occlusion, AR objects may appear to "float" unnaturally in front of real objects.

Implementing Occlusion in Unity

1. **Enable Depth Data**:

   - Configure the AR Camera Manager to enable depth data.

2. **Create a Depth Mask Material**:

   - Use shaders to create materials that mask virtual objects based on depth data.

Real-World Example: Building an AR Measuring Tool

Let's combine these features into a practical example: an AR measuring tool. This app will allow users to measure the distance between two points in their environment.

Objective

Create an AR app where users tap to place two points and display the distance between them in meters.

Step 1: Setting Up the Scene

1. **Create a New Project**:

   o Open Unity and create a new 3D project.

2. **Add AR Session and AR Session Origin**:

   o Add **AR Session** and **AR Session Origin** to the scene.

   o Include the AR Plane Manager and AR Raycast Manager components.

Step 2: Adding Measurement Points

1. **Create a 3D Sphere**:
   - In the Hierarchy, right-click and select **3D Object > Sphere**.
   - Scale it down to represent a point marker.
   - Save it as a Prefab.

2. **Create a Line Renderer**:
   - Right-click in the Hierarchy and select **Effects > Line Renderer**.
   - Configure the Line Renderer to draw a line between two points.

Step 3: Writing the Measurement Script

1. **Create a Script**:
   - Right-click in the Assets folder, select **Create > C# Script**, and name it ARMeasureTool.

2. **Add the Following Code**:

csharp

Copy code

```
using UnityEngine;

using UnityEngine.XR.ARFoundation;

using UnityEngine.XR.ARSubsystems;
```

```csharp
using System.Collections.Generic;

public class ARMeasureTool : MonoBehaviour
{
    public GameObject pointPrefab;
    public LineRenderer lineRenderer;
    private List<Vector3> points = new
List<Vector3>();
    private ARRaycastManager raycastManager;

    void Start()
    {
        raycastManager =
FindObjectOfType<ARRaycastManager>();
    }

    void Update()
    {
        if (Input.touchCount > 0)
        {
            Touch touch = Input.GetTouch(0);
```

```csharp
            if (touch.phase == TouchPhase.Began)
            {
                List<ARRaycastHit> hits = new
List<ARRaycastHit>();
                if (raycastManager.Raycast(touch.position,
hits, TrackableType.PlaneWithinPolygon))
                {
                    Pose hitPose = hits[0].pose;
                    PlacePoint(hitPose.position);
                }
            }
        }
    }


    void PlacePoint(Vector3 position)
    {
        Instantiate(pointPrefab, position,
Quaternion.identity);
        points.Add(position);


        if (points.Count == 2)
```

```
{
    lineRenderer.SetPosition(0, points[0]);
    lineRenderer.SetPosition(1, points[1]);


    float distance = Vector3.Distance(points[0], points[1]);
    Debug.Log($"Distance: {distance} meters");
    }
  }
}
```

Step 4: Testing the Tool

1. **Assign Prefabs and Components**:
   - Attach the script to the AR Session Origin.
   - Assign the point Prefab and Line Renderer in the Inspector.

2. **Deploy to a Device**:
   - Build and run the project on an Android or iOS device.
   - Test by tapping two points on a detected plane to measure the distance.

This chapter delved into essential AR features like plane detection, image recognition, and environmental understanding. By applying these tools, you can create immersive, functional AR applications. The AR measuring tool is a practical example that showcases how these features can be integrated to solve real-world problems.

Part 3: Advanced AR Development

7. AR in 3D Space

Building immersive AR experiences involves working with 3D models, physics, and animations to create realistic and engaging interactions. This chapter explores how to optimize 3D models for mobile AR, integrate physics and animations into AR objects, and culminates in a real-world example: developing a simple AR basketball game.

Optimizing 3D Models for Mobile AR

AR applications typically run on mobile devices, which have limited processing power compared to PCs or gaming consoles. Optimizing 3D models ensures smooth performance while maintaining visual fidelity.

1. Model Optimization

- **Polygon Count**: Reduce the polygon count of 3D models while retaining their shape and details.

  - Use tools like Blender or Maya to simplify meshes.

  - Aim for low-poly models for mobile AR while keeping a balance between performance and aesthetics.

- **Texture Resolution**: Optimize texture sizes to reduce memory usage.

  - Use textures with resolutions no higher than required (e.g., 512x512 or 1024x1024 for mobile).

2. Material Optimization

- Limit the number of materials and shaders applied to a single object.

- Use Unity's **Mobile Standard Shader**, which is optimized for low-power devices.

- Consider **baking lighting** into textures for static objects to reduce real-time lighting calculations.

3. Asset Compression

- Use Unity's **Import Settings** to compress textures, reduce file sizes, and optimize mesh data.

- Enable **Mipmap generation** for textures to improve rendering at varying distances.

4. Level of Detail (LOD)

- Implement LOD groups for complex models to adjust their detail based on the user's distance.

- Use highly detailed models when close to the camera and switch to simpler models as they move farther away.

Adding Physics and Animations to AR Objects

To make AR experiences more interactive, integrating physics and animations is key. Physics makes objects behave realistically, while animations add life and movement to the scene.

1. Physics in Unity

Unity's physics system allows you to simulate real-world behaviors like gravity, collisions, and forces.

Components for Physics

- **Rigidbody**: Adds physical properties like mass, gravity, and drag.

- **Collider**: Defines the physical boundaries of an object.

- **Physics Materials**: Control friction and bounciness of surfaces.

Example: Adding Gravity

To apply gravity to a virtual basketball:

1. Add a **Rigidbody** component to the basketball object.

2. Configure its properties:

    o Enable **Use Gravity**.

    o Adjust **Mass** for realistic motion.

csharp

Copy code

```csharp
Rigidbody rb = basketball.GetComponent<Rigidbody>();

rb.useGravity = true;

rb.mass = 0.6f; // Approximate mass of a basketball
```

2. Animations in Unity

Animations can be created directly in Unity or imported from external tools like Blender or Maya.

Unity's Animator System

- Use the **Animator Controller** to define and manage animations for objects.

- Create transitions between animation states based on triggers or conditions.

Example: Animating a Basketball Hoop

1. Create an animation for the hoop net using Unity's Animation window.

2. Add an **Animator Component** to the hoop.

3. Control the animation programmatically:

csharp

Copy code

```csharp
Animator animator =
hoop.GetComponent<Animator>();

animator.SetTrigger("Swish"); // Trigger net animation
when a basket is scored
```

Real-World Example: A Simple AR Basketball Game

Now, let's apply these concepts to create a fun and interactive AR basketball game. The game will involve throwing a virtual basketball into a hoop placed in the real-world environment.

Objective

Develop an AR basketball game where:

1. Players tap the screen to launch a basketball.

2. The basketball interacts with the environment using physics.

3. A score is recorded when the ball passes through the hoop.

Step 1: Setting Up the Scene

1. **Create a New Unity Project**:

   - o Open Unity and create a new 3D project.

   - o Set the target platform to Android or iOS.

2. **Add AR Session and AR Session Origin**:

   - o Right-click in the **Hierarchy** and select **XR > AR Session Origin**.

   - o Add **AR Session** to manage AR functionality.

Step 2: Adding Game Elements

1. **Create a Basketball Prefab**:

   - o Import a basketball 3D model or create a sphere in Unity.

   - o Add a **Rigidbody** and a **Sphere Collider** to simulate physics.

   - o Save it as a Prefab.

2. **Create a Basketball Hoop**:

   - o Import or create a 3D hoop model with a backboard.

- Add a **Box Collider** to the backboard and a **Mesh Collider** to the hoop for accurate physics.

- Save it as a Prefab.

3. **Add a Plane Manager**:

- Select the AR Session Origin and add an **AR Plane Manager** component to detect flat surfaces.

- Visualize the planes using a semi-transparent material.

Step 3: Writing the Basketball Shooting Script

Create a script to handle basketball spawning and shooting mechanics.

1. **Create a New Script**:

- Right-click in the Assets folder, select **Create > C# Script**, and name it BasketballShooter.

2. **Add the Following Code**:

csharp

Copy code

using UnityEngine;

```
using UnityEngine.XR.ARFoundation;

using UnityEngine.XR.ARSubsystems;

using System.Collections.Generic;


public class BasketballShooter : MonoBehaviour
{
    public GameObject basketballPrefab;

    public Transform spawnPoint;

    public float shootForce = 500f;

    private ARRaycastManager raycastManager;

    private List<ARRaycastHit> hits = new
List<ARRaycastHit>();


    void Start()
    {
        raycastManager =
FindObjectOfType<ARRaycastManager>();
    }


    void Update()
    {
```

```
    if (Input.touchCount > 0)

    {

        Touch touch = Input.GetTouch(0);

        if (touch.phase == TouchPhase.Began)

        {

            ShootBasketball();

        }

    }

}


    void ShootBasketball()

    {

        GameObject basketball =
Instantiate(basketballPrefab, spawnPoint.position,
spawnPoint.rotation);

        Rigidbody rb =
basketball.GetComponent<Rigidbody>();

        rb.AddForce(spawnPoint.forward * shootForce);

    }

}
```

3. **Configure the Script**:

- Attach the script to the AR Session Origin.

- Assign the basketball Prefab and specify the spawn point.

Step 4: Adding Scoring Logic

1. **Create a Score Manager**:
   - Create a new script called ScoreManager and attach it to an empty GameObject.

2. **Add the Following Code**:

csharp

Copy code

```csharp
using UnityEngine;


public class ScoreManager : MonoBehaviour
{
    public int score = 0;
```

```csharp
    public void AddScore()
    {
        score++;
        Debug.Log("Score: " + score);
    }
}
```

3. **Detect Hoop Collisions**:
   - Add a trigger collider to the hoop.
   - Create a script to detect when the ball passes through:

csharp

Copy code

```csharp
using UnityEngine;

public class HoopTrigger : MonoBehaviour
{
    public ScoreManager scoreManager;

    void OnTriggerEnter(Collider other)
    {
```

```
if (other.CompareTag("Basketball"))

    {

        scoreManager.AddScore();

        Destroy(other.gameObject); // Remove the
basketball after scoring

    }

  }

}
```

4. **Tag the Basketball**:
   - Assign the tag "Basketball" to the basketball Prefab.

Step 5: Testing the Game

1. **Deploy to Device**:
   - Build and run the project on an Android or iOS device.

2. **Test Gameplay**:
   - Launch the app and aim the camera at a flat surface.
   - Place the hoop using AR plane detection.
   - Tap the screen to shoot basketballs and score points.

This chapter demonstrated how to optimize 3D models for mobile AR, integrate physics and animations, and apply these concepts to create an AR basketball game. By combining Unity's physics system, animation tools, and AR Foundation, you can craft engaging and interactive experiences.

In the next chapter, we'll explore spatial mapping and world-building techniques to enhance AR environments further. Keep pushing your AR development skills to the next level!

8. Spatial Mapping and World Building

Spatial mapping and world building are essential for crafting immersive AR experiences. By understanding and mapping real-world spaces, developers can dynamically place virtual objects and enable navigation through AR environments. This chapter will explore how to map spaces, place objects dynamically, and guide users in a real-world example: creating an AR treasure hunt.

Mapping Real-World Spaces in AR

What is Spatial Mapping?

Spatial mapping is the process of capturing and representing real-world geometry in AR. This data enables AR applications to:

- Understand the dimensions and features of the environment.

- Interact with physical spaces realistically.

- Provide context-aware experiences, such as placing objects on detected surfaces or behind real-world obstacles.

How Spatial Mapping Works

1. **Sensor Data**:

   o AR devices use cameras, depth sensors, and gyroscopes to collect data about the physical environment.

2. **Point Clouds**:

   o Sensors generate a "point cloud," a collection of 3D points that represent surfaces in the environment.

3. **Plane Detection**:

   o Algorithms analyze point clouds to identify flat surfaces, such as floors, walls, and tables.

4. **Depth Understanding**:

   o Depth APIs provide a measure of how far objects are from the camera, allowing AR objects to interact with real-world geometry (e.g., occlusion).

Unity Tools for Spatial Mapping

Unity's **AR Plane Manager** and **AR Raycast Manager** are the primary tools for implementing spatial mapping. Additionally, ARCore and ARKit support advanced features like environmental depth.

Implementing Spatial Mapping

1. Add the **AR Plane Manager** to your AR Session Origin to detect and track real-world surfaces.

2. Use the **AR Raycast Manager** to determine where users tap within the AR environment.

Dynamic Object Placement and Navigation

Dynamic Object Placement

Dynamic object placement allows users to interact with AR by placing virtual items in specific locations based on the real-world context.

Example Workflow for Object Placement

1. **Surface Detection**:

   o Use the AR Plane Manager to detect surfaces.

2. **Raycasting**:

   o Cast a ray from the user's touch point to find a valid surface.

3. **Instantiate Objects**:

- o Place objects at the intersection of the ray and the detected plane.

Here's a simple script for dynamic object placement:

csharp

Copy code

```csharp
using UnityEngine;

using UnityEngine.XR.ARFoundation;

using UnityEngine.XR.ARSubsystems;

using System.Collections.Generic;


public class DynamicPlacement : MonoBehaviour
{

    public GameObject objectToPlace;

    private ARRaycastManager raycastManager;

    private List<ARRaycastHit> hits = new
List<ARRaycastHit>();


    void Start()
    {

        raycastManager =
GetComponent<ARRaycastManager>();

    }
```

```
void Update()
{
    if (Input.touchCount > 0)
    {
        Touch touch = Input.GetTouch(0);
        if (touch.phase == TouchPhase.Began)
        {
            if (raycastManager.Raycast(touch.position,
hits, TrackableType.PlaneWithinPolygon))
            {
                Pose hitPose = hits[0].pose;
                Instantiate(objectToPlace,
hitPose.position, hitPose.rotation);
            }
        }
    }
}
```

Navigation in AR

Navigation involves guiding users through AR environments to specific locations or virtual objects. This can be achieved by:

1. **Anchors**:

    o Use AR anchors to ensure virtual objects remain in specific locations relative to the real world.

2. **Waypoints**:

    o Create virtual markers that guide users to the target.

3. **AR Paths**:

    o Generate visual paths (e.g., arrows or lines) that indicate the direction to navigate.

Real-World Example: Creating an AR Treasure Hunt

Objective

Develop an AR treasure hunt game where users explore a mapped environment to find virtual treasure chests. The game involves:

1. Placing treasure chests dynamically in the AR environment.

2. Guiding users to the treasure using visual cues.

3. Rewarding users upon finding and opening the treasure.

Step 1: Setting Up the Scene

1. **Create a New Unity Project**:

    o Open Unity and create a new 3D project.

2. **Add AR Session and AR Session Origin**:

    o Right-click in the **Hierarchy** and select **XR > AR Session Origin**.

    o Add **AR Session** to manage AR functionality.

3. **Enable Plane Detection**:

    o Add the **AR Plane Manager** to the AR Session Origin to detect real-world surfaces.

4. **Add Raycast Support**:

    o Attach the **AR Raycast Manager** to handle user interactions.

Step 2: Designing the Treasure Hunt

1. **Create Treasure Chest Prefab**:

- Import or create a 3D model of a treasure chest.

- Add a **Box Collider** to the model for detecting interactions.

- Save the model as a Prefab.

2. **Design a Visual Cue (Waypoint)**:

- Create a simple visual marker (e.g., an arrow or glowing sphere) to guide users to the treasure chest.

- Save it as a Prefab for reuse.

Step 3: Writing the Treasure Placement Script

1. **Create a Script**:

- Right-click in the Assets folder, select **Create > C# Script**, and name it TreasureHuntManager.

2. **Add the Following Code**:

csharp

Copy code

```
using UnityEngine;

using UnityEngine.XR.ARFoundation;

using UnityEngine.XR.ARSubsystems;
```

```csharp
using System.Collections.Generic;

public class TreasureHuntManager : MonoBehaviour
{
    public GameObject treasurePrefab;
    public GameObject waypointPrefab;
    private ARRaycastManager raycastManager;
    private List<ARRaycastHit> hits = new
List<ARRaycastHit>();


    void Start()
    {
        raycastManager =
GetComponent<ARRaycastManager>();
    }


    public void PlaceTreasure()
    {
        if (raycastManager.Raycast(new
Vector2(Screen.width / 2, Screen.height / 2), hits,
TrackableType.PlaneWithinPolygon))
        {
```

```csharp
        Pose hitPose = hits[0].pose;

        Instantiate(treasurePrefab, hitPose.position,
hitPose.rotation);


        // Place a waypoint near the treasure

        Vector3 waypointPosition = hitPose.position +
new Vector3(0, 0.2f, 0);

        Instantiate(waypointPrefab, waypointPosition,
Quaternion.identity);

    }

  }

}
```

3. **Trigger Treasure Placement**:

   o Add a button in Unity's UI to allow users
      to place a treasure.

Step 4: Adding Interaction

1. **Open the Treasure Chest**:

   o Add an interaction script to the treasure
      chest Prefab:

csharp

Copy code

```csharp
using UnityEngine;

public class TreasureChest : MonoBehaviour
{
    private bool isOpened = false;

    void OnMouseDown()
    {
        if (!isOpened)
        {
            Debug.Log("You found the treasure!");
            isOpened = true;
            OpenChest();
        }
    }

    void OpenChest()
    {
        // Play an animation or display rewards

        GetComponent<Animator>().SetTrigger("Open");
```

}

}

2. **Animation**:

   o Create an opening animation for the
      chest using Unity's Animation window.

Step 5: Adding Navigation Cues

1. **Place Waypoints**:

   o Use the TreasureHuntManager script to
      dynamically position waypoints near the
      treasure.

2. **Highlight the Path**:

   o Add glowing effects or an animated line
      to guide users.

Step 6: Testing the Treasure Hunt

1. **Build and Deploy**:

   o Build and run the app on an Android or
      iOS device.

2. **Play the Game**:

o   Place a treasure chest in the AR
    environment.

o   Use visual cues to locate and interact
    with the chest.

This chapter explored spatial mapping, dynamic object placement, and navigation techniques in AR. By creating an AR treasure hunt, you've applied these concepts to a fun and interactive project that engages users with real-world spaces.

In the next chapter, we'll expand on lighting, shadows, and environmental effects to make AR objects blend seamlessly into the real world. Keep building and enhancing your AR skills!

9. Lighting and Shadows in AR

Lighting and shadows play a critical role in creating believable AR experiences. Realistic lighting ensures that virtual objects appear to be part of the real-world environment, while shadows help ground objects in space. This chapter explores how to use Unity's light estimation, match virtual shadows to real-world environments, and create a practical example: a virtual lamp that blends with room lighting.

Realistic Lighting: Using Unity's Light Estimation

Realistic lighting in AR involves making virtual objects respond to the real-world lighting conditions captured by the device's camera and sensors. Unity's **AR Foundation** supports light estimation, which dynamically adjusts virtual lighting based on the environment.

How Light Estimation Works

AR Foundation gathers environmental light data through ARCore or ARKit and provides values for:

- **Ambient Intensity**: The brightness of the environment.

- **Color Temperature**: The warmth or coolness of the light (measured in Kelvin).

These values can then be used to adjust virtual lighting in the scene.

Implementing Light Estimation in Unity

1. **Add Light Estimation to the Scene**:

   o Select the **AR Camera** in your AR Session Origin.

   o Add the **AR Camera Manager** component.

   o Enable the **Light Estimation** feature.

2. **Use a Script to Update Lighting**:

   o Create a script to dynamically update the intensity and color of a directional light based on the light estimation data.

csharp

Copy code

```
using UnityEngine;

using UnityEngine.XR.ARFoundation;
```

```csharp
public class LightEstimation : MonoBehaviour
{
    public Light sceneLight;
    private ARCameraManager cameraManager;

    void Start()
    {
        cameraManager =
FindObjectOfType<ARCameraManager>();
    }

    void Update()
    {
        if (cameraManager.TryGetLightEstimation(out
ARLightEstimationData lightData))
        {
            if (lightData.averageBrightness.HasValue)
            {
                sceneLight.intensity =
lightData.averageBrightness.Value;
            }
```

```
        if (lightData.colorTemperature.HasValue)

        {

            sceneLight.colorTemperature =
lightData.colorTemperature.Value;

        }

      }

    }

}
```

3. **Assign the Script**:

   o Attach the script to an empty
      GameObject and assign your scene's
      directional light to the sceneLight field.

Matching Virtual Shadows with Real-World Environments

Shadows are crucial for grounding virtual objects in AR. Without them, objects may appear to float unnaturally. Unity offers several techniques to create realistic shadows in AR.

1. Using Shadow Casters

Shadow casters are virtual objects that project shadows onto the AR environment.

- **Steps**:

    o Add a **Directional Light** to your scene and ensure it casts shadows.

    o Enable **Shadows** in the AR Plane Manager to allow planes to receive shadows.

2. Using Shadow Receivers

Shadow receivers are invisible planes that capture and display shadows to simulate interaction with the real-world environment.

- **Steps**:

    1. Create a **Shadow Plane**:

        ▪ Add a plane to your scene and scale it appropriately.

        ▪ Use a transparent material with a **Shadow Caster** shader to make the plane invisible while still displaying shadows.

    2. Assign the Shadow Plane:

        ▪ Place the shadow plane beneath your virtual objects.

3. Adjusting Shadow Quality

- In Unity's **Quality Settings**, adjust shadow resolution, distance, and softness to match the AR experience's performance and realism.

Example Shadow Shader

Create a material for shadows using the **Shadow Caster** shader. This material will only display the shadows cast by virtual objects.

Real-World Example: A Virtual Lamp That Blends with Room Lighting

Now, let's create a virtual lamp that dynamically adjusts to room lighting and casts realistic shadows on a detected surface.

Objective

Build an AR experience where:

1. A virtual lamp is placed on a detected surface.

2. The lamp's light responds to real-world brightness and color temperature.

3. The lamp casts realistic shadows on the AR environment.

Step 1: Setting Up the Scene

1. **Create a New Project**:

   o   Open Unity and create a new 3D project.

2. **Add AR Session and AR Session Origin**:

   o   Right-click in the **Hierarchy** and select **XR > AR Session Origin**.

   o   Add **AR Session** to manage AR functionality.

3. **Enable Plane Detection**:

   o   Add the **AR Plane Manager** to the AR Session Origin.

Step 2: Designing the Virtual Lamp

1. **Create a Lamp Model**:

   o   Import or create a 3D model of a lamp.

   o   Ensure the lamp has a **Point Light** component to simulate its glow.

2. **Adjust the Light Properties**:

   o   Set the intensity, range, and color of the Point Light for the desired effect.

3. **Save as a Prefab**:

   o   Drag the lamp object into the **Assets** folder to create a Prefab.

Step 3: Writing the Lighting Script

1. **Create a Script**:

   - Right-click in the Assets folder, select **Create > C# Script**, and name it LampLightController.

2. **Add the Following Code**:

csharp

Copy code

```
using UnityEngine;

using UnityEngine.XR.ARFoundation;


public class LampLightController : MonoBehaviour

{

    public Light lampLight;

    public Light sceneLight;

    private ARCameraManager cameraManager;


    void Start()

    {

        cameraManager =
FindObjectOfType<ARCameraManager>();
```

```
    }


    void Update()

    {

        if (cameraManager.TryGetLightEstimation(out
ARLightEstimationData lightData))

        {

            if (lightData.averageBrightness.HasValue)

            {

                sceneLight.intensity =
lightData.averageBrightness.Value;

                lampLight.intensity =
lightData.averageBrightness.Value * 0.5f; // Adjust
lamp brightness proportionally

            }

            if (lightData.colorTemperature.HasValue)

            {

                sceneLight.colorTemperature =
lightData.colorTemperature.Value;

                lampLight.colorTemperature =
lightData.colorTemperature.Value;

            }

        }
```

```
        }

}
```

3. **Assign the Script**:

   o Attach the script to the lamp Prefab.

   o Assign the Point Light and the
      Directional Light to the respective fields
      in the Inspector.

Step 4: Adding Shadows

1. **Create a Shadow Plane**:

   o Add a plane to your scene beneath the
      lamp.

   o Assign a transparent material with a
      Shadow Caster shader to this plane.

2. **Enable Shadows on the Lamp**:

   o Ensure the Point Light in the lamp casts
      shadows.

   o Adjust the shadow settings for softness
      and resolution.

Step 5: Placing the Lamp Dynamically

1. **Add Placement Functionality**:

- o Create a script to place the lamp on a detected surface.

csharp

Copy code

```csharp
using UnityEngine;

using UnityEngine.XR.ARFoundation;

using UnityEngine.XR.ARSubsystems;

using System.Collections.Generic;


public class LampPlacement : MonoBehaviour
{
    public GameObject lampPrefab;

    private ARRaycastManager raycastManager;

    private List<ARRaycastHit> hits = new
List<ARRaycastHit>();


    void Start()
    {
        raycastManager =
GetComponent<ARRaycastManager>();
    }
```

```csharp
void Update()
{
    if (Input.touchCount > 0)
    {
        Touch touch = Input.GetTouch(0);
        if (touch.phase == TouchPhase.Began)
        {
            if (raycastManager.Raycast(touch.position,
hits, TrackableType.PlaneWithinPolygon))
            {
                Pose hitPose = hits[0].pose;
                Instantiate(lampPrefab, hitPose.position,
hitPose.rotation);
            }
        }
    }
}
```

2. **Attach the Script**:
   - Add the script to the AR Session Origin.

Step 6: Testing the Lamp

1. **Build and Deploy**:

    o   Build and run the app on an Android or iOS device.

2. **Test Placement and Lighting**:

    o   Place the lamp on a detected surface.

    o   Observe how the lamp's light and shadows respond to real-world lighting.

Lighting and shadows are critical for creating realistic AR experiences. By leveraging Unity's light estimation and shadow tools, you can ensure your virtual objects blend seamlessly with the real world. The virtual lamp example showcases how these techniques come together to create a compelling and interactive AR application.

Part 4: AR in Practice

10. Integrating AR with Backend Systems

Augmented Reality (AR) experiences are greatly enhanced when integrated with backend systems. By saving and loading AR sessions and syncing data with cloud services, you can create persistent and collaborative AR applications. This chapter explores these concepts and demonstrates a real-world example: building a shared AR experience using Firebase.

Saving and Loading AR Sessions

What Is AR Session Persistence?

AR session persistence enables users to save the state of their AR experience and resume it later. This includes saving:

- The positions and states of virtual objects.

- Anchors tied to specific locations in the real world.

- User-specific data such as scores or progress in an AR game.

How to Save AR Sessions

Saving AR sessions typically involves:

1. **Serializing AR Data**:

   - Convert AR object data (e.g., positions, orientations, and properties) into a storable format like JSON.

2. **Storing the Data**:

   - Save serialized data locally (e.g., on the device) or remotely (e.g., in a cloud database).

Unity Example: Saving and Loading Data Locally

Here's a simple example to save and load the positions of AR objects:

1. **Saving Object Data**:

csharp

Copy code

```csharp
[System.Serializable]
public class ARObjectData
{
    public Vector3 position;
    public Quaternion rotation;
}
```

```csharp
public class ARSessionManager : MonoBehaviour
{
    public GameObject arObject;

    public void SaveARSession()
    {
        ARObjectData data = new ARObjectData
        {
            position = arObject.transform.position,
            rotation = arObject.transform.rotation
        };

        string jsonData = JsonUtility.ToJson(data);
        PlayerPrefs.SetString("ARSessionData", jsonData);
    }
}
```

2. **Loading Object Data**:

csharp

Copy code

```
public void LoadARSession()

{

    string jsonData =
PlayerPrefs.GetString("ARSessionData", null);


    if (!string.IsNullOrEmpty(jsonData))

    {

        ARObjectData data =
JsonUtility.FromJson<ARObjectData>(jsonData);

        arObject.transform.position = data.position;

        arObject.transform.rotation = data.rotation;

    }

}
```

Advanced: Storing Anchors

For persistent placement of AR objects in the physical world, store anchor data (e.g., AR planes or anchors) alongside object data. Unity's AR Foundation provides APIs for creating and managing anchors.

Syncing AR Experiences with Cloud Services

Why Sync AR with the Cloud?

Cloud services enable shared AR experiences, collaborative features, and session persistence across devices. Key benefits include:

- Multi-user AR interactions.

- Access to session data from any device.

- Real-time synchronization of AR object states.

Choosing a Cloud Service

Popular cloud services for AR integration include:

- **Firebase Realtime Database**: Offers real-time data synchronization.

- **Amazon Web Services (AWS)**: Provides scalable backend solutions.

- **Google Cloud**: Integrates with ARCore for advanced features.

Firebase for AR Syncing

Firebase is a powerful backend service that simplifies real-time data synchronization. It's an excellent choice for collaborative AR experiences.

Firebase Realtime Database Integration

1. **Set Up Firebase in Unity**:

   o Install the Firebase Unity SDK.

- Configure your Firebase project in the Firebase Console.
- Download and import the google-services.json (for Android) or GoogleService-Info.plist (for iOS).

2. **Real-Time Data Handling**:

- Use the Firebase Database API to write and retrieve data.
- Implement event listeners for real-time updates.

Example: Syncing Object Positions

Here's how to sync AR object positions with Firebase:

1. **Writing to Firebase**:

```csharp
Copy code
using Firebase.Database;
using UnityEngine;

public class FirebaseManager : MonoBehaviour
{
```

```csharp
private DatabaseReference dbReference;

void Start()
{
    dbReference =
FirebaseDatabase.DefaultInstance.RootReference;
}


public void UpdateObjectPosition(string objectId,
Vector3 position)
{

dbReference.Child("ARObjects").Child(objectId).Chil
d("position").SetValueAsync(new
    {
        x = position.x,
        y = position.y,
        z = position.z
    });
}
}
```

2. **Listening for Updates**:

```csharp
Copy code
public void ListenForObjectUpdates(string objectId,
Transform arObject)
{

dbReference.Child("ARObjects").Child(objectId).Chil
d("position").ValueChanged += (sender, args) =>
    {
        if (args.DatabaseError == null)
        {
            var positionData = args.Snapshot.Value as
Dictionary<string, object>;
            Vector3 newPosition = new Vector3(
                float.Parse(positionData["x"].ToString()),
                float.Parse(positionData["y"].ToString()),
                float.Parse(positionData["z"].ToString())
            );
            arObject.position = newPosition;
        }
    };
}
```

Real-World Example: A Shared AR Experience Using Firebase

Objective

Develop an AR application where multiple users can collaborate in the same virtual space. Users will:

1. Place AR objects dynamically.

2. See changes made by others in real-time.

3. Use Firebase to sync object positions across devices.

Step 1: Setting Up Firebase

1. **Create a Firebase Project**:

   o Go to the Firebase Console.

   o Create a new project and add your Unity app.

2. **Enable Realtime Database**:

   o In the Firebase Console, navigate to **Build > Realtime Database**.

   o Set the database rules to allow read/write access for development (restrict for production).

3. **Import Firebase SDK**:

   - ○ Download and import the Firebase Unity SDK.

   - ○ Configure the project with the required google-services.json or GoogleService-Info.plist.

Step 2: Building the AR Application

1. **Create a Unity Scene**:

   - ○ Add **AR Session** and **AR Session Origin**.

   - ○ Include the AR Plane Manager for surface detection.

2. **Add Object Placement**:

   - ○ Allow users to place AR objects on detected surfaces using the following script:

csharp

Copy code

```
public class ARSharedPlacement : MonoBehaviour
{
    public GameObject objectPrefab;
```

```csharp
private ARRaycastManager raycastManager;

void Start()
{
    raycastManager =
GetComponent<ARRaycastManager>();
}

void Update()
{
    if (Input.touchCount > 0)
    {
        Touch touch = Input.GetTouch(0);
        if (touch.phase == TouchPhase.Began)
        {
            List<ARRaycastHit> hits = new
List<ARRaycastHit>();

            if (raycastManager.Raycast(touch.position,
hits, TrackableType.PlaneWithinPolygon))
            {
                Pose hitPose = hits[0].pose;
                PlaceObject(hitPose);
```

```
            }
        }
    }
}


    void PlaceObject(Pose hitPose)

    {

        GameObject placedObject =
Instantiate(objectPrefab, hitPose.position,
hitPose.rotation);


FirebaseManager.Instance.UpdateObjectPosition("Obj
ectID", placedObject.transform.position);

    }
}
```

Step 3: Syncing AR Objects

1. **Initialize Firebase Manager**:

   o Create a singleton for managing Firebase
     operations:

csharp

Copy code

```csharp
public class FirebaseManager : MonoBehaviour
{
    public static FirebaseManager Instance;
    private DatabaseReference dbReference;

    void Awake()
    {
        if (Instance == null)
        {
            Instance = this;
            DontDestroyOnLoad(gameObject);
        }
    }

    void Start()
    {
        dbReference =
FirebaseDatabase.DefaultInstance.RootReference;
    }
```

```csharp
    public void UpdateObjectPosition(string objectId,
Vector3 position)

    {


dbReference.Child("ARObjects").Child(objectId).Chil
d("position").SetValueAsync(new

        {

            x = position.x,

            y = position.y,

            z = position.z

        });

    }

}
```

2. **Listen for Changes**:

   o   Sync object positions across users:

csharp

Copy code

```csharp
public void ListenForChanges(string objectId,
Transform arObject)

{


dbReference.Child("ARObjects").Child(objectId).Chil
d("position").ValueChanged += (sender, args) =>
```

```
{
    if (args.DatabaseError == null)
    {
        var posData = args.Snapshot.Value as
Dictionary<string, object>;
        arObject.position = new Vector3(
            float.Parse(posData["x"].ToString()),
            float.Parse(posData["y"].ToString()),
            float.Parse(posData["z"].ToString())
        );
    }
};
}
```

Step 4: Testing the Shared Experience

1. **Deploy to Multiple Devices**:
   - Build and deploy the app to two or more devices.
   - Ensure Firebase is configured correctly.

2. **Collaborate in AR**:
   - Place objects in one device's AR environment.

- Observe real-time updates on the other device(s).

Integrating AR with backend systems like Firebase unlocks powerful capabilities for saving, loading, and sharing AR experiences. By synchronizing AR object states across devices, you can enable collaborative and persistent AR applications.

The shared AR experience example demonstrated the practical application of these techniques, paving the way for complex, interactive, and scalable AR solutions. Next, we'll explore how to optimize AR performance and prepare your app for deployment. Keep building!

11. UI/UX Design for AR

Creating intuitive and engaging user interfaces (UI) and user experiences (UX) is essential for the success of any AR application. In AR, the interface extends beyond traditional 2D screens into the 3D physical environment, requiring unique design considerations. This chapter covers the principles of designing AR interfaces, best practices for user engagement, and a practical example: building a tutorial overlay for new AR users.

Designing Intuitive AR Interfaces

AR interfaces need to balance simplicity with functionality, ensuring users can navigate the augmented environment without confusion. Here are key principles to follow:

1. Reduce Cognitive Load

- Avoid overwhelming users with excessive UI elements or complex interactions.

- Guide users step-by-step, providing only the necessary information for each stage.

2. Leverage Familiar Interactions

- Use gestures like tap, swipe, and pinch, which are familiar to most mobile users.

- Incorporate real-world metaphors, such as dragging objects to move them or pinching to resize.

3. Design for Spatial Awareness

- Place UI elements within the user's field of view.

- Use spatial cues, such as arrows or glowing markers, to guide users to points of interest.

4. Combine 2D and 3D UI Elements

- Use 2D elements (e.g., menus, buttons) for settings and instructions.

- Use 3D elements (e.g., holograms, indicators) for in-world interactions.

5. Provide Feedback

- Offer visual and auditory feedback for user actions, such as sounds when an object is placed or animations when a task is completed.

Best Practices for User Engagement in AR Apps

AR engagement relies on seamless interaction and maintaining user interest. Follow these best practices:

1. Onboarding and Tutorials

- Provide a clear and interactive tutorial to introduce users to the app's features.

- Highlight key gestures or interactions needed to navigate the AR environment.

2. Context-Aware Interactions

- Use environment-specific interactions, such as only allowing object placement on detected surfaces.

- Adapt the app's behavior to the user's surroundings, like changing lighting or object appearance based on ambient light.

3. Persistent Elements

- Keep critical elements like action buttons or tooltips easily accessible.

- Use anchors to ensure virtual objects remain in place as users move.

4. Encourage Exploration

- Incorporate gamification elements, like rewards or challenges, to motivate users to interact with the AR environment.

- Allow users to customize or manipulate virtual objects.

5. Maintain Performance

- Optimize assets and interactions to ensure smooth performance, as lag or stuttering can break immersion.

Real-World Example: A Tutorial Overlay for New AR Users

An effective tutorial is crucial for onboarding users who are new to AR. Let's create a tutorial overlay that guides users through the basics of using an AR app, including:

1. Scanning the environment.

2. Placing an object on a detected surface.

3. Interacting with the object.

Step 1: Setting Up the Scene

1. **Create a New Unity Project**:

- o Open Unity and create a 3D project.
- o Set up the AR Session and AR Session Origin as usual.

2. **Enable Plane Detection**:

  - o Add the AR Plane Manager to detect and visualize real-world surfaces.

3. **Add UI Elements**:

  - o Add a **Canvas** to the scene and set it to **Screen Space - Overlay**.

Step 2: Designing the Tutorial UI

1. **Create a Message Panel**:

  - o Add a **Panel** to the Canvas for displaying instructions.
  - o Add a **Text** element inside the panel to display tutorial messages.

2. **Add Navigation Buttons**:

  - o Add two buttons: **Next** and **Skip**.
  - o Style them with labels and icons for clarity.

3. **Add Visual Indicators**:

  - o Create a 3D arrow or glowing sphere to guide users in the AR environment.

- Save it as a Prefab.

Step 3: Writing the Tutorial Script

1. **Create a Script**:
   - Right-click in the Assets folder, select **Create > C# Script**, and name it ARTutorial.

2. **Add the Following Code**:

csharp

Copy code

```csharp
using UnityEngine;
using UnityEngine.UI;

public class ARTutorial : MonoBehaviour
{
    public Text tutorialText;
    public GameObject indicatorPrefab;
    private int tutorialStep = 0;

    void Start()
    {
```

```csharp
        ShowStep(tutorialStep);
    }

    public void NextStep()
    {
        tutorialStep++;
        ShowStep(tutorialStep);
    }

    public void SkipTutorial()
    {
        tutorialText.gameObject.SetActive(false);
        // Hide other tutorial elements
    }

    private void ShowStep(int step)
    {
        switch (step)
        {
            case 0:
```

```
            tutorialText.text = "Welcome! Move your
device to scan the environment.";

            break;

        case 1:

            tutorialText.text = "Tap on a detected
surface to place an object.";

            PlaceIndicator();

            break;

        case 2:

            tutorialText.text = "Great! Now interact with
the object.";

            break;

        default:

            tutorialText.text = "You're ready to
explore!";

            SkipTutorial();

            break;

        }

    }


    private void PlaceIndicator()

    {
```

```csharp
Vector3 indicatorPosition = new Vector3(0, 0, 1);
// Example position

Instantiate(indicatorPrefab, indicatorPosition, Quaternion.identity);
    }
}
```

3. **Assign the Script**:

   - Attach the script to an empty GameObject in the scene.

   - Link the UI elements (e.g., Text and Buttons) to the script in the Inspector.

Step 4: Integrating AR Interactions

1. **Add Raycasting for Object Placement**:

   - Extend the tutorial to detect surfaces and place objects dynamically.

csharp

Copy code

```csharp
using UnityEngine;

using UnityEngine.XR.ARFoundation;

using UnityEngine.XR.ARSubsystems;

using System.Collections.Generic;
```

```csharp
public class ARPlacement : MonoBehaviour
{
    public GameObject objectPrefab;
    private ARRaycastManager raycastManager;
    private List<ARRaycastHit> hits = new
List<ARRaycastHit>();

    void Start()
    {
        raycastManager =
FindObjectOfType<ARRaycastManager>();
    }

    void Update()
    {
        if (Input.touchCount > 0)
        {
            Touch touch = Input.GetTouch(0);

            if (touch.phase == TouchPhase.Began)
```

```
        {

            if (raycastManager.Raycast(touch.position,
hits, TrackableType.PlaneWithinPolygon))

                {

                    Pose hitPose = hits[0].pose;

                    Instantiate(objectPrefab, hitPose.position,
hitPose.rotation);

                }

            }

        }

    }

}
```

2. **Combine with the Tutorial**:
   - Link the placement functionality to a specific tutorial step.

Step 5: Testing and Polishing

1. **Build and Deploy**:
   - Build and run the app on a device to test the tutorial in an AR environment.

2. **Refine Visuals**:

   o   Adjust the size and position of UI
       elements for readability.

   o   Add animations or transitions for tutorial
       steps.

3. **Gather Feedback**:

   o   Test with users to identify pain points
       and improve clarity.

Designing intuitive AR interfaces and engaging experiences requires careful consideration of both traditional UI elements and spatial interactions. By creating a tutorial overlay, you've learned how to onboard users effectively and guide them through AR features. This foundation can be extended to build more complex, user-friendly AR applications.

In the next chapter, we'll explore debugging and testing techniques to ensure your AR app runs smoothly across various devices. Keep building your AR expertise!

12. Debugging and Testing AR Apps

Debugging and testing are critical steps in AR development to ensure smooth functionality and a seamless user experience. AR apps often involve complex interactions between hardware, software, and real-world environments, making thorough testing essential. In this chapter, we'll explore methods for testing AR apps on real devices, debugging tips for tracking and gestures, and a real-world example of diagnosing and fixing misplaced AR objects.

Testing AR Apps on Real Devices

Why Test on Real Devices?

Simulators and emulators provide a controlled environment for early testing, but they lack the capabilities of real AR devices, such as:

- Camera input for real-world environments.

- Depth sensors for spatial mapping.

- Accelerometers and gyroscopes for motion tracking.

Testing on actual devices ensures that your app performs well under realistic conditions.

Steps for Testing on Devices

1. **Prepare Your AR Device**:

    o Ensure that the device supports ARCore (Android) or ARKit (iOS).

    o Enable Developer Options and USB Debugging (Android) or use Xcode provisioning profiles (iOS).

2. **Build and Deploy Your App**:

    o For Android:

        ▪ Connect your device via USB.

        ▪ In Unity, go to **File > Build Settings**, select **Android**, and click **Build and Run**.

    o For iOS:

        ▪ Open the project in Xcode after building.

        ▪ Connect your device and deploy the app via Xcode.

3. **Test in Varied Environments**:

- o Evaluate the app's performance in different lighting conditions, surface types, and spatial configurations.

4. **Log and Monitor**:

   - o Use Unity's **Debug.Log** to capture runtime information.

   - o Monitor device performance using profiling tools (e.g., Unity Profiler or Android Studio).

Debugging Tips for AR Features

AR apps rely on precise tracking, gesture recognition, and environmental understanding. Here are debugging strategies for common issues:

1. Tracking Issues

Tracking issues arise when the app fails to recognize or maintain an accurate understanding of the real-world environment.

Symptoms:

- Virtual objects drift or appear misaligned with the real world.

- Plane detection is slow or inaccurate.

Solutions:

- **Optimize Environment Scanning**:

  - Ensure the testing environment has sufficient light and distinct textures.

  - Avoid reflective or transparent surfaces, as these can confuse the camera.

- **Improve Performance**:

  - Reduce the number of active AR features (e.g., disable unused planes).

  - Optimize object complexity to lighten computational load.

2. Gesture Recognition Problems

Gestures, such as tap and swipe, may not register correctly.

Symptoms:

- Taps are not detected consistently.

- Gestures trigger unintended actions.

Solutions:

- **Calibrate Touch Input**:

- Log touch positions using Debug.Log(touch.position) to verify their accuracy.

- **Implement Gesture Thresholds**:

  - Use a threshold to filter unintentional touches or minor movements.

csharp

Copy code

```csharp
if (touch.phase == TouchPhase.Moved &&
touch.deltaPosition.magnitude > gestureThreshold)
{
    // Handle swipe gesture
}
```

3. Anchor and Object Placement Errors

Virtual objects may appear in incorrect positions or orientations.

Symptoms:

- Objects are placed in mid-air instead of on detected surfaces.

- Objects rotate or scale unexpectedly.

Solutions:

- **Validate Raycast Hits**:

- o Ensure raycasts detect valid planes before placing objects.

csharp

Copy code

```csharp
if (raycastManager.Raycast(touch.position, hits,
TrackableType.PlaneWithinPolygon))
{
    Pose hitPose = hits[0].pose;

    Instantiate(objectPrefab, hitPose.position,
hitPose.rotation);
}
```

- **Debug Anchor Stability**:
  - o Check anchor stability using AR Foundation's anchor tracking states.

Real-World Example: Fixing an Issue with Misplaced AR Objects

Scenario

You've developed an AR app that places virtual objects on detected surfaces. During testing, users report that objects frequently appear floating in mid-air or far from the intended placement.

Step 1: Investigating the Issue

1. **Reproduce the Bug**:
   - Test the app on different surfaces and lighting conditions to replicate the issue.
   - Observe the placement behavior using debugging tools.

2. **Log Raycast Results**:
   - Add logging to check if raycasts detect valid planes.

csharp

Copy code

```csharp
if (raycastManager.Raycast(touch.position, hits,
TrackableType.PlaneWithinPolygon))
{
    Debug.Log("Raycast hit at: " +
hits[0].pose.position);
}
else
{
    Debug.Log("No valid surface detected.");
```

}

Step 2: Diagnosing the Problem

After analyzing the logs and observations:

- **Finding**: The app attempts to place objects even when no valid surface is detected, resulting in floating or misplaced objects.

Step 3: Fixing the Issue

1. **Validate Surface Detection**:

   - Modify the object placement script to handle invalid raycasts gracefully.

csharp

Copy code

```csharp
if (raycastManager.Raycast(touch.position, hits,
TrackableType.PlaneWithinPolygon))
{
    Pose hitPose = hits[0].pose;

    Instantiate(objectPrefab, hitPose.position,
hitPose.rotation);
}
else
```

```
{

    Debug.LogWarning("No valid surface detected.
Object not placed.");

}
```

2. **Add Visual Feedback**:

    o Use visual indicators, such as a crosshair or outline, to show where the object will be placed.

    o Update the indicator only when a valid surface is detected.

csharp

Copy code

```
indicator.SetActive(raycastManager.Raycast(touch.position, hits, TrackableType.PlaneWithinPolygon));

if (indicator.activeSelf)

{

    indicator.transform.position = hits[0].pose.position;

}
```

Step 4: Testing the Fix

1. **Rebuild and Deploy**:

    o Implement the updated script and deploy the app to a device.

2. **Test Scenarios**:

- o Test in environments with:

    - Varying surface textures and sizes.

    - Challenging conditions (e.g., low light, cluttered backgrounds).

3. **Validate Results**:

- o Confirm that objects are only placed on valid surfaces and remain aligned with the real-world environment.

Step 5: Optimizing Placement Experience

1. **Enhance Placement Accuracy**:

- o Add a delay to allow plane detection to stabilize before placing objects.

csharp

Copy code

```csharp
IEnumerator PlaceObjectWithDelay(Vector3 position,
Quaternion rotation)
{
    yield return new WaitForSeconds(0.5f);
    Instantiate(objectPrefab, position, rotation);
}
```

2. **Provide User Feedback**:

    o   Display a message if no valid surface is detected, guiding the user to move the camera or find a better area.

Debugging and testing AR apps involve addressing unique challenges like tracking errors, gesture recognition issues, and environmental variability. By systematically identifying and resolving these problems, you can ensure a polished and reliable AR experience.

The real-world example of fixing misplaced objects demonstrates how to diagnose and resolve common AR placement issues, making your apps more intuitive and user-friendly. In the next chapter, we'll explore best practices for optimizing AR app performance and preparing your project for deployment. Keep refining your AR skills!

Part 5: Publishing and Scaling Your AR App

13. Optimizing Performance for Mobile AR

Optimizing performance is critical for ensuring smooth and enjoyable AR experiences, especially on mobile devices with limited resources. Mobile AR apps must balance functionality, graphical quality, and resource consumption. This chapter explores techniques for reducing power and memory usage, alongside strategies to maintain smooth performance, even on older devices.

Reducing Power and Memory Usage in AR Apps

1. Optimize 3D Models and Assets

Simplify 3D Models

- **Lower Polygon Count**: Use low-poly models that maintain visual fidelity while reducing computational overhead.

- **Level of Detail (LOD)**: Implement LOD groups to use simpler models when objects are farther from the camera.

Compress Textures and Materials

- Resize large textures to a resolution suitable for mobile devices (e.g., 512x512 or 1024x1024).

- Use compressed texture formats like **ETC2** for Android or **ASTC** for cross-platform efficiency.

Reuse Materials

- Share materials across multiple objects instead of creating duplicates to reduce memory consumption.

2. Manage Lighting and Shadows

Bake Lighting

- Use precomputed lighting (baked lighting) for static objects to eliminate the need for real-time lighting calculations.

Use Light Estimation Wisely

- Leverage Unity's AR light estimation only when necessary. Disable it for static or minimally dynamic scenes to save processing power.

Simplify Shadows

- Use **soft shadows** sparingly, as they are computationally expensive.

- Apply **blob shadows** (simple circular shadows under objects) to mimic depth without rendering complex shadow maps.

3. Optimize Physics Simulations

Limit Physics Objects

- Minimize the number of objects with **Rigidbody** or Collider components to reduce physics calculations.

Adjust Fixed Timestep

- Increase Unity's **Fixed Timestep** interval (default is 0.02 seconds) to reduce the frequency of physics updates.

4. Optimize Code and Scripts

Minimize Update Calls

- Avoid heavy computations in the **Update()** method. Use event-driven programming or coroutines for non-critical operations.

Pool Objects

- Implement object pooling to reuse GameObjects instead of instantiating and destroying them repeatedly.

```csharp
csharp

Copy code

// Example Object Pooling

public class ObjectPool : MonoBehaviour
{
    public GameObject prefab;
    private Queue<GameObject> pool = new Queue<GameObject>();

    public GameObject GetObject()
    {
        if (pool.Count > 0)
        {
            GameObject obj = pool.Dequeue();
            obj.SetActive(true);
            return obj;
        }
        return Instantiate(prefab);
    }

    public void ReturnObject(GameObject obj)
```

```
    {
        obj.SetActive(false);
        pool.Enqueue(obj);
    }
}
```

5. Optimize Memory Management

Unload Unused Assets

- Use Resources.UnloadUnusedAssets() to free memory allocated to unused assets.

Reduce Texture Memory

- Limit the number of active textures in the scene.

- Use **Texture Atlases** to combine multiple textures into one, reducing draw calls.

Avoid Large Object Hierarchies

- Flatten GameObject hierarchies to reduce the complexity of scene graphs.

6. Monitor Power Consumption

Reduce Camera Usage

- Minimize the use of additional cameras. Rely primarily on the AR camera to process visual data.

Optimize AR Sessions

- Stop unnecessary AR subsystems (like plane detection or image tracking) when not in use.

csharp

Copy code

// Example: Stop Plane Detection

arPlaneManager.enabled = false;

Limit Framerate

- Cap the app's frame rate to 30 FPS for non-intensive AR experiences to save battery life.

Strategies for Smooth AR Experiences on Older Devices

1. Device-Specific Optimization

Target Appropriate Hardware

- Use Unity's **Graphics API settings** to exclude features unsupported by older devices (e.g., Vulkan for Android devices lacking Vulkan support).

Profile Performance

- Test and profile your app using Unity's **Profiler** and external tools like Android Studio or Xcode Instruments.

- Identify bottlenecks and address specific issues on underperforming devices.

2. Reduce Rendering Overhead

Limit Draw Calls

- Minimize the number of objects and materials rendered at a time.

- Use batching (static or dynamic) to combine draw calls for similar objects.

Lower Shader Complexity

- Use mobile-friendly shaders and avoid effects like real-time reflections or complex transparency.

Reduce Post-Processing

- Avoid or minimize post-processing effects like bloom, motion blur, and anti-aliasing, which can significantly impact performance.

Dynamic Resolution Scaling

- Adjust rendering resolution dynamically based on the device's performance.

csharp

Copy code

```
Screen.SetResolution(Screen.width / 2, Screen.height / 2, true);
```

3. Optimize Environmental Features

Simplify Plane Detection

- Limit plane detection to horizontal or vertical planes based on app requirements.

- Use smaller bounding boxes to constrain the area scanned by the AR session.

Optimize Object Placement

- Implement feedback mechanisms (like a preview or indicator) to reduce invalid placement attempts and unnecessary calculations.

Use Object Occlusion Wisely

- If occlusion is required, use depth-based occlusion only when essential to minimize processing demands.

4. Adapt to User Context

Simplify Interactions

- Use gestures and interactions that require fewer resources (e.g., taps instead of continuous drags).

Offer Quality Settings

- Provide users with options to adjust graphic quality, lighting, and effects based on their device capabilities.

csharp

Copy code

```csharp
public void SetQuality(int level)
{
    QualitySettings.SetQualityLevel(level);
}
```

5. Ensure Stability

Handle Edge Cases

- Test and optimize your app for scenarios like low-light conditions, cluttered environments, and reflective surfaces.

Provide Feedback for Failures

- Inform users when features like plane detection or tracking are unavailable due to environmental conditions.

Real-World Example: Optimizing an AR App for Older Devices

Scenario

You've built an AR app that allows users to place virtual furniture in their homes. While the app performs well on newer devices, users with older devices report:

1. Laggy interactions.

2. Slow plane detection.

3. Excessive battery drain during usage.

Step 1: Identify Performance Bottlenecks

1. **Profile the App**:

   o Use Unity's **Profiler** to analyze:

     ▪ CPU usage: High due to frequent plane detection updates.

     ▪ GPU usage: High due to complex 3D models and real-time shadows.

2. **Test on Target Devices**:

   o Deploy the app to older devices and monitor user feedback.

- o Confirm the bottlenecks in performance under constrained hardware.

Step 2: Apply Optimizations

1. **Simplify Plane Detection**:
   - o Disable vertical plane detection to reduce computational load.

csharp

Copy code

```csharp
arPlaneManager.detectionMode = PlaneDetectionMode.Horizontal;
```

2. **Reduce Model Complexity**:
   - o Simplify 3D furniture models by reducing polygon count and compressing textures.
   - o Replace high-resolution materials with a texture atlas.

3. **Optimize Lighting**:
   - o Replace real-time shadows with baked lighting for static objects.
   - o Use blob shadows for dynamic objects like chairs.

4. **Cap Frame Rate:**

- Limit the frame rate to 30 FPS for smoother performance.

csharp

Copy code

Application.targetFrameRate = 30;

5. **Add Quality Settings**:
   - Provide users with a toggle to reduce graphic quality on older devices.

csharp

Copy code

```csharp
public void ToggleLowQuality(bool isLowQuality)
{
    if (isLowQuality)
    {
        QualitySettings.SetQualityLevel(0);
    }
    else
    {
        QualitySettings.SetQualityLevel(2);
    }
}
```

Step 3: Retest and Validate

1. **Deploy Updated App**:

     o Test the optimized app on older devices.

2. **Measure Improvements**:

     o Verify improved responsiveness during interactions.

     o Ensure reduced lag during plane detection and object placement.

3. **Collect Feedback**:

     o Gather user feedback to ensure the changes enhance the user experience without sacrificing too much functionality.

Optimizing performance for mobile AR apps is a critical step in ensuring smooth interactions and broad accessibility. By reducing power and memory usage, simplifying rendering and interactions, and applying device-specific strategies, you can significantly improve performance on older devices.

The example of optimizing an AR furniture app demonstrates how thoughtful adjustments can transform the user experience. In the next chapter, we'll explore how to publish your AR app effectively, preparing it for app stores and scaling to a wider audience. Keep refining your AR projects!

14. Publishing Your AR App

Publishing your AR app involves preparing it for distribution, ensuring compliance with ARCore and ARKit requirements, and crafting effective marketing strategies to reach your target audience. This chapter will guide you through the process of deploying your app to the App Store and Google Play, meeting AR compliance standards, and promoting your AR app for success.

Preparing Your App for App Store and Google Play

1. Preparing for Google Play (Android)

Google Play is the primary distribution platform for Android apps. Follow these steps to prepare your AR app for publication:

Step 1: Configure Your Build Settings

1. Open Unity and navigate to **File > Build Settings**.

2. Select **Android** as your platform and click **Switch Platform**.

3. Ensure **ARCore Support** is enabled:

   o Go to **Edit > Project Settings > XR Plug-in Management** and enable **ARCore**.

4. Adjust the **Player Settings**:

   o Under **Resolution and Presentation**, set the default orientation (e.g., portrait or landscape).

   o Under **Other Settings**, set:

      ▪ **Minimum API Level** to at least **Android 7.0 (API level 24)**, required for ARCore.

      ▪ **Target API Level** to the latest supported version.

   o Add a unique **Package Name** (e.g., com.yourcompany.arapp).

Step 2: Generate a Keystore

Google Play requires all apps to be signed with a keystore:

1. Open **Edit > Project Settings > Player > Publishing Settings**.

2. Check **Custom Keystore** and create a new keystore file.

3. Save the keystore securely for future updates.

Step 3: Build the APK or AAB

1. Return to **Build Settings**.

2. Select **Build** or **Build and Run** to generate an APK or AAB file.

Step 4: Test Your App

- Use Google Play's **Internal Testing Track** to upload your APK/AAB and gather feedback from testers.

---

2. Preparing for the App Store (iOS)

The App Store is Apple's distribution platform for iOS apps. Follow these steps to prepare your AR app for publication:

Step 1: Configure Your Build Settings

1. Open Unity and navigate to **File > Build Settings**.

2. Select **iOS** as your platform and click **Switch Platform**.

3. Ensure **ARKit Support** is enabled:

   o Go to **Edit > Project Settings > XR Plug-in Management** and enable **ARKit**.

4. Adjust the **Player Settings**:

- Set your **Bundle Identifier** (e.g., com.yourcompany.arapp).

- Enable **Automatically Sign** and provide your Apple Developer credentials.

Step 2: Build the Xcode Project

1. In Unity, click **Build and Run** to generate an Xcode project.

2. Open the project in Xcode.

Step 3: Test on a Physical Device

- Use a provisioning profile to test your app on an iPhone or iPad.

Step 4: Submit to the App Store

1. In Xcode, select **Product > Archive**.

2. Use the **Organizer** window to upload your app to the App Store.

3. Complete the submission process in App Store Connect, including metadata, screenshots, and compliance information.

ARCore and ARKit Compliance Requirements

ARCore Compliance

Google's ARCore SDK has specific requirements for apps:

1. **Device Compatibility**:

   o Ensure your app targets ARCore-supported devices. A list of compatible devices is available on the ARCore website.

2. **Permissions**:

   o Request **Camera** and **Motion Sensor** permissions in the app manifest.

3. **Performance Testing**:

   o Test thoroughly for plane detection, light estimation, and tracking stability.

4. **ARCore Services**:

   o Ensure ARCore Services are installed and up to date on the user's device.

ARKit Compliance

Apple's ARKit SDK has its own requirements:

1. **Device Compatibility**:

   o Ensure your app runs on ARKit-supported devices, such as iPhones and iPads with A9 chips or later.

2. **Privacy Requirements**:

- o Include **NSCameraUsageDescription** in your app's Info.plist file, explaining why the app requires camera access.

3. **Design Guidelines**:

- o Follow Apple's Human Interface Guidelines for AR to ensure a smooth user experience.

Marketing Your AR App: Real-World Strategies

Launching your app successfully requires effective marketing strategies to reach and engage your audience. Here are practical approaches to promote your AR app:

1. Build a Compelling Product Page

The product page on the App Store and Google Play is often the first interaction users have with your app. Optimize it for maximum impact:

- **App Name**: Choose a descriptive and memorable name.

- **Description**: Highlight your app's unique AR features and benefits.

- **Screenshots and Videos**: Showcase key functionalities like object placement, interaction, or special effects.

- **Keywords**: Include AR-related terms to improve discoverability.

2. Create a Teaser Video

- Develop a short, engaging video that demonstrates the core features of your AR app.

- Highlight its immersive capabilities, such as object manipulation, spatial interactions, or real-world integration.

3. Leverage Social Media

Use platforms like Instagram, TikTok, and Twitter to showcase AR features and user-generated content:

- Share videos of your app in action.

- Encourage users to post their own AR creations with branded hashtags.

4. Collaborate with Influencers

- Partner with content creators or tech reviewers who focus on AR, gaming, or app development.

- Provide them with early access to your app in exchange for reviews or tutorials.

5. Offer Incentives

- Launch with promotions such as free trials, discounts, or exclusive in-app content for early adopters.

- Gamify your app with challenges or rewards to encourage engagement.

6. Engage Your Users

- Build a community around your app by interacting with users on forums, social media, or through an in-app feedback system.

- Update your app regularly with new features or content to retain users.

Real-World Example: Marketing a Virtual Home Design App

Scenario

You've developed an AR app that allows users to place virtual furniture in their homes and visualize room designs. Your goal is to launch and promote the app effectively.

Step 1: Optimize the Product Page

- App Name: **"AR Home Designer: Plan Your Space"**.

- Description: "Reimagine your living space with AR Home Designer. Place virtual furniture, experiment with layouts, and visualize your dream home in real-time."
- Screenshots:
    - Showcase a chair placed on a detected floor.
    - Highlight customization features, such as changing furniture colors or layouts.

Step 2: Create a Promotional Video

- Record a short demo:
    - Show the app scanning a room.
    - Highlight a user placing a virtual sofa and customizing its color.
    - End with a transformation of the room into a fully furnished design.

Step 3: Promote on Social Media

- Share "before and after" videos on Instagram and TikTok.
- Encourage users to share their designs using hashtags like **#ARHomeDesigner**.

Step 4: Collaborate with Home Décor Influencers

- Partner with interior design influencers to showcase your app.

- Provide them with free access and ask them to share their experiences.

Step 5: Engage Users with Challenges

- Launch a **"Best Room Design"** contest with prizes for the most creative layouts.

- Feature winning designs on your website and social media.

Publishing an AR app involves more than just uploading it to the App Store or Google Play. It requires meticulous preparation, adherence to compliance requirements, and strategic marketing efforts. By optimizing your app for distribution and implementing creative promotional strategies, you can reach a wide audience and maximize its impact.

In the next chapter, we'll explore the future of AR development, discussing emerging trends and opportunities for innovation. Keep building and scaling your AR app to new heights!

15. The Future of AR Development

The future of augmented reality (AR) holds immense promise, with advancements in hardware, software, and connectivity pushing the boundaries of what's possible. In this chapter, we'll explore emerging trends like AR glasses and 5G, Unity's pivotal role in shaping AR's future, and the transformative potential of AR across industries. By envisioning what's ahead, readers can position themselves to lead in this rapidly evolving field.

Emerging Trends: AR Glasses, 5G, and Beyond

1. AR Glasses: The Next Frontier

While mobile devices have been the primary platform for AR, the next major leap is AR glasses. These wearable devices offer hands-free, immersive experiences that integrate digital elements directly into the user's field of view.

Current Developments

- **Consumer-Focused Glasses**:
  - Companies like **Snap** (Spectacles), **Nreal**, and **Rokid** have introduced AR glasses aimed at everyday users.
- **Enterprise Solutions**:
  - **Microsoft HoloLens** and **Magic Leap** focus on industrial applications like training, remote collaboration, and design.

Potential Applications

- **Productivity**:
  - AR glasses can revolutionize workflows by overlaying instructions, blueprints, or annotations in real-world contexts.
- **Gaming**:
  - Fully immersive AR games that blend seamlessly with physical spaces.
- **Healthcare**:
  - Real-time visualization of medical data during surgeries or diagnostics.

Challenges

- Miniaturizing hardware without compromising functionality.

- Achieving widespread adoption by reducing costs and improving aesthetics.

---

2. 5G: Empowering Real-Time AR

The rollout of 5G networks is a game-changer for AR, addressing many of the latency and bandwidth challenges associated with real-time AR applications.

Advantages of 5G for AR

- **Low Latency**:
    - AR applications like remote collaboration and live gaming require near-instantaneous responses, achievable with 5G's sub-10ms latency.

- **High Bandwidth**:
    - 5G supports large-scale AR experiences, such as streaming high-quality 3D content directly to devices.

- **Edge Computing**:
    - With 5G, much of the computational workload can be offloaded to edge servers, reducing the strain on mobile devices and enabling lighter, more efficient hardware.

5G-Driven Innovations

- **Shared AR**:

- Multi-user experiences where participants interact with the same AR objects in real-time.

- **Location-Based AR:**

  - AR applications that anchor virtual elements to specific geolocations, enhanced by 5G's precision and speed.

---

3. Beyond 5G: AI and AR Fusion

Artificial Intelligence (AI) is increasingly intertwined with AR, enabling smarter and more intuitive interactions.

AI-Powered Features

- **Object Recognition:**

  - AI algorithms can identify objects in the real world, making AR interactions context-aware.

- **Semantic Understanding:**

  - AR systems can interpret environments, distinguishing between walls, floors, and objects for better placement and interaction.

- **Dynamic Content Generation:**

  - AI can create personalized AR experiences, such as generating virtual furniture layouts tailored to a user's preferences.

AR Cloud:

The AR Cloud is a persistent, shared digital layer over the physical world, enabling global-scale AR experiences. By leveraging cloud computing, AR developers can:

- Anchor objects that remain in place even when users leave and return.

- Create shared environments for collaborative AR applications.

The Role of Unity in Shaping the Future of AR

1. Unity as an AR Development Powerhouse

Unity is at the forefront of AR development, providing tools and frameworks that empower developers to create cutting-edge experiences.

AR Foundation:

Unity's AR Foundation abstracts the complexities of ARCore (Android) and ARKit (iOS), enabling cross-platform development with a single codebase.

Real-Time Rendering:

Unity's rendering engine delivers high-quality visuals, essential for immersive AR applications.

XR Interaction Toolkit:

This toolkit simplifies the creation of interactive AR experiences by providing prebuilt components for common interactions.

2. Emerging Unity Features for AR

- **Unity Mars**:
    - Unity Mars (Mixed and Augmented Reality Studio) simplifies the creation of context-aware AR experiences. It allows developers to simulate real-world environments during development and adapt AR content dynamically to user surroundings.

- **Visual Scripting**:
    - Unity's visual scripting tools make AR development accessible to creators without coding experience, democratizing AR content creation.

3. Unity's Role in Education and Accessibility

Unity's extensive documentation, tutorials, and community resources make it the go-to platform for AR developers at all skill levels. Its accessibility accelerates innovation across industries, from entertainment to education.

Inspiring Readers with the Potential of AR

Transforming Industries with AR

Healthcare:

- **Training and Simulations**:
  - AR enables immersive medical training, allowing students to practice procedures in realistic virtual environments.

- **Augmented Surgery**:
  - Surgeons can visualize internal structures overlaid on patients in real-time, improving precision.

Education:

- **Interactive Learning**:
  - AR brings abstract concepts to life. Students can explore 3D models of planets, molecules, or historical artifacts in their physical space.

- **Skill Development**:

- AR-based simulations provide hands-on experience in fields like engineering, aviation, and architecture.

Retail:

- **Virtual Try-Ons**:
    - Customers can try on clothing, eyewear, or makeup virtually, enhancing convenience and reducing returns.

- **AR Showrooms**:
    - Retailers can display entire product catalogs in compact spaces using AR.

Entertainment and Gaming:

- AR has revolutionized gaming with location-based experiences like **Pokémon Go** and immersive storytelling in apps like **The Walking Dead: Our World**.

- Future AR games will integrate with physical environments even more seamlessly, offering richer, multi-layered experiences.

AR for Social Good

Accessibility:

- AR apps can assist visually impaired users by describing their surroundings in real-time.

- AR sign language interpreters can bridge communication gaps for hearing-impaired individuals.

Environmental Awareness:

- AR can visualize the impact of climate change, enabling users to see rising sea levels or deforestation in their surroundings.

Community Building:

- Shared AR experiences can foster social connections, from collaborative games to global-scale art installations.

Envisioning the Future

Imagine a future where:

- Architects use AR glasses to design and visualize buildings in real-time on-site.

- Students across the globe collaborate on science experiments in a shared AR environment.

- Families explore the history of their neighborhoods through AR-reconstructed scenes from the past.

AR has the potential to enrich every aspect of life, making the invisible visible and transforming how we learn, play, and connect.

The future of AR development is bright and expansive, driven by technological advances like AR glasses, 5G, and AI. Unity will continue to play a pivotal role in enabling developers to push the boundaries of what's possible, fostering innovation across industries.

By embracing these trends and leveraging Unity's tools, you can create experiences that not only entertain but also educate, inspire, and improve lives. As AR technology evolves, the possibilities are limited only by imagination—making now the perfect time to be a part of this transformative field.

Let your creativity guide you, and remember: the future of AR is in your hands!

www.ingramcontent.com/pod-product-compliance
Lightning Source LLC
LaVergne TN
LVHW022344060326
832902LV00022B/4234